BREAKING VICIOUS CIRCLES

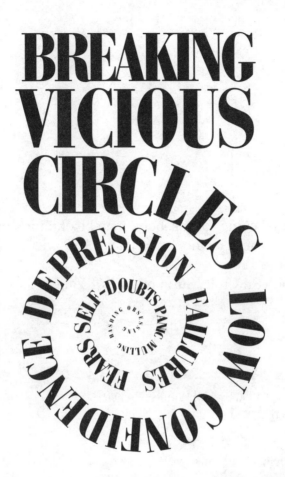

DEPRESSION
LOW CONFIDENCE
FAILURES
FEARS
SELF-DOUBTS
PANIC
OBSESSIVE
BRISING
BELLING

by H.J. Wahler, Ph.D.

Sky Island Press
Sumner, Washington

Additional copies of this book may be obtained by
sending a check or money order for $9.95 per book to:
Sky Island Press
12513 44th St. Ct. E., Sumner, WA 98390

Published by Sky Island Press,
12513 44th St. Ct. E., Sumner, WA 98390

Printed in the United States of America.

Library of Congress Catalog Card No. 89-092750
ISBN: 0-9625926-0-9

Acknowledgements

To my wife, Betty, goes my undying gratitude for her expertise, encouragement and untiring efforts to improve and clarify the different kinds of information this book intends to communicate.

In the same vein, I deeply appreciate my daughter Anita's considerable editorial talents and assistance.

Our efforts could not have come to fruition without the invaluable expertise of professionals in the field of publication. I am very grateful for Deborah Batjer's unflagging editing, formating and electronic typesetting preparations and a spiral cover concept. Jeff Johnson's "Artworks" drawings are excellent graphic illustrations of important issues with a light touch.

Kelly Pensell's inspirations created the format, color scheme and the graphic portrayal of vicious circles endlessly spiraling for the cover. Sheryn Hara, our marketing consultant, has just begun her work. All that she has begun holds great promise for finding and alerting audiences with potential interests in the information that this book contains. The extensive expertise of Elliott Wolf, Publisher of Peanut Butter Publishing, has enabled us to put all our efforts together and produce this book. To each of these invaluable contributors, I extend my most heartfelt appreciation.

Dedication

This book is dedicated to the many people I know who learned to see for themselves.

About the Author

Early in his career as a clinical psycologist, Dr. Wahler became disturbed by the jumbled semantics and contradictory theories that permeated the mental health field. As a scientist, he felt that a clearer picture of the dynamics of emotional problem-solving was both neccessary and possible. He has dedicated the past three decades to the reconciliation of abstract science with pure common sense.

This journey began with clinical and research applications as a graduate student at the University of Iowa. Further experience was gained in dealing with diverse client problems - social, marital, physical disabilities and psychoses - while he served on the teaching staff of Ohio State University and as a consultant to the Ohio Rehabilitation Center. Later, as Director of Psychological Research with the Washington Mental Health Research Institute, he obtained two federal grants that enabled him to investigate community resources and their accessibility by troubled people.

Author of scores of professional papers and articles, Dr. Wahler is well known for his Self-Description and Physical Symptoms Inventories, which have enjoyed wide professional acceptance since the early seventies. His dynamic, simplified techniques of pattern-breaking through self-knowledge can be mastered and implemented by anyone who is trapped by personal vicious circles and wishes to be freed from them.

Contents

Prepare thyself, for thou wilt have to travel on alone. The guide can but point the way.

-Words from *The Voice of the Silence*

CHAPTER 1

*I*ntroduction

We humans are remarkable beings. Certainly this is not because of our superior physical strength, great speed or acute senses. We have become such remarkable creatures because of the relatively recent evolution of our new brains. Our old brains, which manage vital physiological processes, are not superior to comparable brains of other species. The very large cerebral cortex that evolved around the old brain is the new brain that is responsible for our transcendence.

Our new brains provide certain mental capabilities that surpass those of all other creatures. Among them are our superior memory and learning capacities. These capabilities, in turn, are greatly facilitated by our ability to represent and communicate information by means of symbolic systems such as language. All that has been discovered, sensed, inferred, invented or imagined can be represented with language, drawings, mathematics and other symbolic means. Information is the true staff of all life. In this most vital realm, we are uniquely endowed.

Like other creatures, we continually take in information through our senses and learn from observations and personal experiences. But on an entirely different plane, our advanced knowledge and skills are not due to the superior mental capabilities of each person, but rather to the fact that these capabilties have made it possible for cumulative knowledge through the ages to be transmitted from generation to generation.

Our unique mental capabilities, however, exact a price. They leave us vulnerable to puzzling personal problems that do not plague other creatures. These troubling problems take various forms and can grow and persist without our understanding the causes.

Common symptoms of such personal difficulties include fears, depression, bewilderment, bodily distresses, intense and prolonged emotional arousal, reduced effectiveness, impaired relations with others and spontaneous thought that mulls, rehashes and broods.

Current psychiatric criteria hold that there are no organic causes for such disorders. In addition, those experiencing them are described as having "intact reality testing abilities." Nothing is wrong with their brains. No brain damage, brain disease, retardation or psychosis (insanity) is involved. Anyone afflicted with such disorders is normal physically and mentally. Nevertheless the suffering is very real.

People troubled with these uniquely human maladies are acutely aware of their symptoms. They also are aware of environmental distresses, such as those in marital, social, occupational and financial areas. But strangely, they are unaware, or only vaguely aware, of mental and other processes within themselves that are causing the problems to persist.

Many theories have been devised to account for these phenomena, theories about how such problems originated and why people are unaware of what perpetuates them. Best known of these are the theories of Freud who proposed that neuroses, as they were called in his time, were caused by conflicts and traumas in early childhood. He believed that sufferers were unaware (unconscious) of causes and perpetuating processes because such information was repressed into an unconscious mind. In his view, repressed child-

2

hood traumas must be made conscious and re-experienced if sufferers are to recover from their neuroses.

Nevertheless, when we look closely, we find features of our unique mental advantages that contribute to our vulnerabilities. In particular, our versatile memories and abilities to represent information symbolically can be both great assets and liabilities.

We are vulnerable in that our memories will retain information indiscriminately, regardless of its validity or value. In addition, our symbolic abilities in no way guarantee the soundness of our ideas and interpretations. Beliefs in memory influence our interpretations. Our interpretations reinforce our beliefs. Both can mislead, misrepresent and delude us, thus forming self-perpetuating vicious circles.

Like all creatures, we learn and live by sensory information. We know it hurts, for example, when sticks and stones are breaking our bones. Unlike other creatures, however, we are profoundly influenced by symbolic implants – by how we have been indoctrinated, how we have been judged, what we have been told, and what we tell ourselves. These influences can hurt us in more subtle ways that fester.

Further complicating matters is the fact that our memories cannot discriminate between diabolical falsehood and gospel truth. They simply accumulate anything that sticks for whatever reasons. As unfortunate beliefs penetrate our thoughts and actions, they strengthen in degree, growing into a system of convictions.

In this way, distorted information about ourselves, others and our environment can affect our minds as insidiously as viruses can infect our bodies. Viruses contain bits of DNA or RNA which can take over normal cells and trick them into making countless replicas of themselves. Distorted beliefs, likewise, can trick normal mental capabilities into reproducing more and more of their clones.

We are especially vulnerable to damaging information when we are young and most prone to absorb without question what we are told. Young children are particularly defenseless against both physical and verbal abuse. How can children who are repeatedly told they are stupid, wrong or no good develop confidence in their capabilities? How can children who are never told

3

they are loved believe they are lovable?

When we are infected with disease viruses, we develop physical symptoms. Similarly, "misinformation viruses" cause emotional symptoms: fears, tensions, frustrations, despair. These feelings attract attention and we are clearly aware of them. But the detrimental beliefs and disturbing interpretations and thoughts that generate the emotional symptoms do not attract attention. Undetected, they remain free to fester and clone themselves.

By a peculiar twist, emotional symptoms tend to reinforce unfortunate beliefs. A school girl, for example, who suffers many self-doubts and believes she is inadequate, is terrified when called upon to recite in class. She reacts, as we all do when we are threatened, with intense emotional arousal. As she anticipates the trembling, stammering, and bumbling that she has previously experienced, the contempt of her peers flashes into her mind. Since she is agonized by such expectations, these humiliating experiences recur spontaneously and augment both her fears and feelings of inferiority.

Self-defeating beliefs grow and persist in perfectly normal brains. Demeaning beliefs create demeaning expectations. Threatening expectations evoke natural emotional reactions which cause disturbing feelings and ineffectual functioning. Intense emotional arousal, in turn, invites perceptions of incompetence that only confirm self-defeating beliefs. Our super brains, memories and symbolic representations provide ideal conditions for such vicious circles to flourish.

Both our bodies and our minds are vulnerable to harmful invasions. But the powers that formed us did not leave our physical bodies to the mercy of microbes, nor leave us incapable of protecting our minds from the ravages of destructive misinformation. A valiant immune system is on guard around the clock protecting our bodies. Our brains, likewise, are armed with capabilities to protect us from the proliferation of crippling misinformation. These two protective systems, however, operate entirely differently.

The immune system is fully automatic. It is continually on guard against harmful intruders. It requires nothing from us except that we maintain our health the best we can. In contrast, our brains

4

do not automatically protect us from implants of detrimental information in memory nor from their proliferation by normal mental processes. We have to *intentionally choose* to identify and protect ourselves from these infections.

We have inborn capabilities that automatically alert us to possible dangers in the environment. We also are equipped with inborn capabilities that enable us to protect ourselves from dangers in our mental world.

Any stimulation out of the ordinary from our environments or bodies spontaneously attracts attention. Such rapid information-seeking tendences are innate and automatic in us and most animals. Clearly they play an essential role in survival.

In contrast, when threatening thoughts and interpretations well up in our minds, they do not automatically attract attention. What attracts our attention are the troubled feelings, such as fear, they are likely to stir up. Being aware of feelings does not mean we are aware of their sources. However, as will be seen later, we are equipped with inborn capabilities that enable us to become clearly aware of information produced by our brains. We have windows in our mental world, but we have to choose to look into them.

We truly feel "born again" when we prove to ourselves that it is within our power to make choices that can gradually shape our lives. Although the future is unknown and the past cannot be changed, we begin to realize that the direction of our lives rests with the succession of choices we make in the present. Our habits cannot be changed by discovering how we acquired them. They change only by changing what perpetuates them in the present. A wonderful security can grow when we give ourselves permission to release the past and focus our energy on structuring the present.

In the following chapters, we will consider the many facets of our remarkable selves. We will look at the powers of our brains that are under our control and see how they can protect us from our vulnerabilities. We will examine the basic features of our minds and their relationships to our bodies and behavior. And to illustrate how we can utilize our innate capabilities to take control of our lives, we will draw upon the real experiences of people who were struggling with a variety of persistent personal problems.

We all have our preferences and ways of going about things. When personal troubles become sufficiently distressful to motivate doing something about them, there are many different paths that people may take. Some will turn to stars, mystics, gurus or cults. Others lie on the couch and explore their repressed childhood traumas. A large number of people will seek new strength from their religion. Many just "tough it out" and do whatever it takes to "feel good."

This book is for people who want self-understanding from facts they can see for themselves. One of its main purposes is to show how we can see for ourselves influences long believed to be unconscious. That we possess these inborn capabilities can be readily proven to ourselves. Seeing this, we can apply our good common sense to gain the understanding that lets us eliminate old spontaneous habits that cause our problems to persist.

$\mathcal{T}$ricks of the Mind
Paranoidal Vicious Circles

We live in time. *Now* is as brief as you want to call it. If it is one trillionth of a second, then *now* vanishes before it is even uttered. Memory is a time bridge linking the past to the present. Perception and thought interpret the present as it unfolds and these processes project into a time that has not yet come.

We live in time, from memory's store of past happenings, to interpretations of the flow of ongoing events, and forward with expectations of what lies ahead. There is room for much error in the store itself; interpretations increase errors, and projections into future time are the least accurate of all. Errors in memory make errors in interpretations and expectations. Worse, errors in interpretations and expectations reinforce errors in memory.

These are the kinds of processes that tormented Clara and induced strange effects. Clara was the second youngest of five children, all fairly close in age. Her rather blurry recollections of her preteen childhood consisted of routines, conformity, a hovering uneasiness and some bits of fun but nothing joyous.

7

Father was an army sergeant who wore his stripes at home. For him life was one-sided. Whatever needed doing had to be done now and done right. Whatever was done right, according to his standards, needed no comment. Whatever was done wrong or too slowly had to be corrected with disparagement or his big buckled belt.

Mother did not help balance the picture. She was more like an obedient child than a mother, going about her chores meticulously and on time, always careful to avoid Father's wrath. Such no-win regimes in childhood, with rigid standards, punishment and no compensating approval or affection, are ripe conditions for establishing in memory uncertainties about one's value and competence.

Clara was not unattractive, but her shyness obscured her charm. School life, like home life, was drab. A few boys showed an interest in her, but this flustered Clara so that their interest soon dwindled. Clara believed that she was on the outside looking in. She suffered feelings that when translated into language came out in statements like, "I'm not as good as others. Nobody likes me. I can't cope like others."

During her eleventh grade, a popular young man named Ken showed an interest in Clara. Ken had shown an interest in quite a few young ladies and Clara could not believe that he fancied her. Because of his dauntless nature, moreover, Ken did not drift away like the others. For several months, his attentions were a source of acute distress. Clara did not know what to say or how to act. She wondered what he saw in her and expected imminent rejection. But as time passed and he lingered, her apprehensions eased somewhat until a new feeling began to emerge. It was so wonderful, it had to be love.

Clara became pregnant. What to do? She hated living at home and was sick of school. She knew her father's reaction would be a disaster. On the other hand, the thought of having her own baby, a person who would be her very own, became a longing. She and Ken talked about marriage. At first the idea stirred an uneasiness in him, but as they shared youthful fantasies about newfound freedoms and joys, the prospect gained appeal. Ken's father was a construction contractor and the trade skills and connections Ken had acquired left no doubt in his mind that they could make it. Ideas gathered about all the good things that awaited them and all the bad ones they would leave behind. They married.

Clara's marriage and baby presented new experiences that sharply contrasted with the conditions under which she had grown up. Before long Ken found work and they moved into their own place. It was like living in a dream. Clara was a mother, homemaker and wife, roles she had thought she would never experience. There was no railing about her shortcomings. Ken was easygoing, appreciative and could be quite affectionate. Bit by bit she became more courageous and even dared to like herself a little. Troubling memories and vague thoughts that it could not last drifted into awareness occasionally, but with baby and homemaking needing her attention, dark reminiscences and apprehensions sank back into the recesses of memory. Although there were the usual frustrations of a struggling young family, there were real satisfactions. Ken got a raise, the house was getting fixed up, baby grew cuter by the day, Ken was never mean and soon a second baby was on the way.

Their life was remarkably free of serious difficulties for nearly two years. But despite the relative contentment, at times Clara felt a foreboding. Qualms crept into her awareness periodically, given impetus by random happenings. Ken was away from home more and it was not always clear where he was. Occasionally he came home very late and would offer flimsy excuses. Clara's qualms were stirring old memories.

Rumors about Ken being a ladies' man were nothing new. Clara's sister had tried to talk with her about it, but Clara not only averted such talk, she also struggled against thinking about it. Despite her best efforts, unanswered questions would not go away. They invited more wondering. Had she just been living in a dream that was ending? What was wrong with her? Her father had never liked her; was Ken now losing interest in her, too?

The more Clara tried not to think, the more doubts and uncertainties dominated her thoughts. She became more watchful for the very things she did not want to see. While doing the laundry, her concerns were fueled by noticing a little red smudge on Ken's shirt collar. She seemed troubled, but would not answer Ken's questions about what was wrong. His irritability and discomfort increased. Clara's suspicions multiplied and Ken grew tired of her moroseness. They were uneasy with one another and became more distant.

Clara's fragmented suspicions burst into a conviction when she found a slip of paper in Ken's shirt pocket with an address, phone number and the name "Sherry." She burst into tears and sank into despairing thought: "Nobody ever loved me. Ken just married me because of the baby." After a few days, she collected herself enough to ask Ken about Sherry. He told her her imagination was running wild and he only made excuses. Whenever she persisted in raising the issue, he became angry, complaining of being mistrusted and nagged. He began staying away from home more often and for longer spells. Again Clara was a defenseless child. Her budding feelings of worth withered, every uncertainty raising more questions to mull.

In spite of this mental turmoil, Clara's children's needs and household necessities demanded her attention and distracted the mulling for brief spells. During such respites, she would try to think about what could be done. Marital advice articles advocated communication but Ken would not communicate about Sherry, some questionable phone calls, and other concerns that had developed. A neighbor who had left her husband and was living on welfare recommended that course, but the thought of fending for herself and the children terrified Clara. Even more unthinkable was the idea of crawling back to her parents. The more Clara dwelt on her dilemmas, the more she seemed hopelessly trapped.

Ken was experiencing conflicts over many things. The children meant a lot to him. Clara was a good wife and he knew how satisfying a good family life could be from his own childhood – more than could ever be possible by sneaking around to girl-friends' places, getting more involved than he intended and having to lie and invent excuses at both ends. After many long discussions with his parents and weighing matters thoroughly, Ken acknowledged his folly and resolved to make amends. He made a clean breast of it to Clara, asked her forgiveness and swore undying devotion and faithfulness.

Ken's about-face failed to restore the tranquility of their early marriage. Clara's old insecurities had been reawakened. Long-standing feelings of vulnerability drifted in, and dreamlike thoughts filled her consciousness with mounting uncertainties; what had happened before could happen again.

When not working, Ken was home, but nothing was the same as it had been. There was tension and wariness. Telling herself that her naivete had been to blame for Ken's earlier trans-gressions, Clara was guarded and waiting for his next betrayal. When he was gone, she conjured up scenes which seemed so real that she could not hide her apprehensions. Having resolved to mend his ways and knowing about Clara's anxiety, Ken became in-creasingly careful to be on time and let her know his whereabouts. Instead of quieting her apprehensions, though, this solicitousness only heightened them. Ken's punctuality and care convinced Clara that he was hiding something. Clara confused facts with her fantasies and became even more vigilant and argumentative.

Beliefs that are repeatedly confirmed, even if only by fantasies, eventually become certainties for the believer. Clara's convictions about Ken's infidelity peaked at times when she felt particularly ineffectual. She would interpret any irregularity as proof that she was right and that Ken was the rogue she imagined. Once when she found unidentifiable lint on the carpet after being away, she assumed it had fallen from the clothes of some woman Ken had been entertaining in her absence. When she confronted him with the "evidence," Ken was angered by her irrationality but deter-mined to reason with her. It was like pleading with the weather. Clara "knew" what had happened and no one could dispel her con-victions.

As similar but more bewildering confrontations occurred, Ken's patience was weakening. Finally, he left after a particularly bruising episode. Upon coming home from shopping, Clara had found a few crumbs of pink candy on their bedspread. Her percep-tion interpreted this as proof that Ken went all the way with a woman while her child was pacified with candy. She "knew" this because her children never ate candy like that.

11

Going to his parents, Ken described Clara's strange behavior and they told him Clara was sick and needed help. He returned the next day to find Clara tearful and haggard from a sleepless night. He cared enough and had enough good sense to refrain from calling her sick, instead prevailing upon her to join him in getting some help for their problems. Clara knew that her feeling so inferior and unloved brought on spells of despair. At the same time, she was convinced that her problems were Ken's fault. Nevertheless, she was so miserable that she was willing to try anything.

They met with a therapist who believed that relationships are only as solid as the individuals involved. Clara's condition was not stable: her self-confidence was low, she was obsessed with both suspicions and finding evidence to support them, and she was bewildered and frightened. These problems needed to be addressed before the marital issues could be explored. Clara agreed to see if the therapist could help her; Ken also agreed to sessions, with a plan to meet as a couple after they understood themselves better.

At the outset, the therapist's goal was to gain an overview of what both Ken and Clara were experiencing. She developed a panoramic view of Clara's past and present life, of her uncorrected interpretations and memories of feeling inadequate, of her warped perception of her worth and her abilities. Clara viewed herself as stupid, and dwelt constantly on her failures: she was a school dropout, her parents did not love her, she had no friends. Ken's arrival in her otherwise empty life had given her a focus she had never found within herself. But his later rejections of her had devastated all that. Though she had become bolder about expressing her feelings when anything aroused her suspicions, this release neither eased her apprehensions nor resolved their problems. She had become consumed with uncertainties and fearful vigilance.

From both their accounts, it was clear that Ken was not physically abusive and that he tended to be conciliatory with his own remorse and renewed interest in retaining his family. Clara's accusations disturbed him, goaded his guilt and dimmed his dream of restoring a happy family life. Further, her strange behavior perplexed him and her remoteness and inaccessibility dampened his affections.

With the silence that increasingly grew between them, neither knew what the other felt. They invented their own explanations and spilled out their frustrations in mutually disturbing behavior.

What could be done? As discussions between Clara and her therapist progressed, Clara began to see more clearly the emptiness and isolation of her life. She began to realize how notions about her limitations had left her entirely dependent on Ken and devoid of other friendships. And for the first time, she was able to consider the possibility that her own ideas might be complicating matters, even more than Ken's proclivities to be a ladies' man. As awareness grew, Clara nonetheless seemed at a loss about what to do to get out of her terrible rut.

Her therapist proposed three activities, all of which at first seemed impossible. But as they jointly explored them more carefully and Ken endorsed the ideas, offering his support, she gradually gained the courage to start.

One approach was group therapy, a safe, first step in learning to communicate with other people and to discover that she was not the only person to experience fears and doubts. Another idea was for Clara to resume and complete her high school education to help overcome the idea that she was stupid, a dropout and a failure. As she felt ready, a logical extension to this plan could include vocational counseling and training. In this sense, she would become familiar with the benevolent side of the larger world, learning that there was a large segment of her community that actually devoted itself to people's growth.

The third strategy involved both Ken and Clara taking stock of their mutual interests and developing plans to apply them. A wide variety of things that couples and families do to widen their vistas and increase their enjoyment was discussed. The tentative plans they developed were feasible, practical steps toward breaking up an obvious but often overlooked vicious circle: nothing ventured is nothing gained. People who do not stretch themselves are fearful and trapped in empty lives. There also was subtle work to be done to learn how to utilize dormant mental capabilities to counterbalance malignant thinking processes.

Talking with her therapist, communicating with new people, making up educational deficiencies, exploring training and vocational opportunities, and seeking new enjoyment with her family and Ken helped ease the intensity of Clara's fear of helplessness. These experiences brought new information to her attention and gave her different viewpoints to contemplate and explore. She also began learning to stop and investigate her interpretations more carefully, question her "facts," and acknowledge that perhaps her "evidence" was only suspicion. She and Ken also began talking to one another more and guessing less about what the other was feeling.

Clara was learning to observe, to see with her senses and to see from her memory. She was learning how to tell the difference between *interpretations* and *descriptions* of what was seen, heard, felt and recalled. She was learning to think of her problems as recurrent episodes, any one of which could be examined at her own pace. Observing troubling episodes from her memory with her therapist helped her sharpen distinctions between descriptions and interpretations.

The episode with the lint, for example, demonstrated this clearly. She described the phases of the episode as they unfolded in time. First she saw a piece of lint which she perceived as different. This was the trigger that automatically released memories of her preoccupations with Ken's unfaithful involvement with other women. She saw how this perception, a flash interpretation, set off emotions of fear and anger and motivated accusations that angered Ken, which she had then further interpreted as proof that she was right.

Troubling episodes had rushed by like a stream, but Clara was learning that after they had run their course she could retrieve them from memory for close examination. She even discovered that at times she could disrupt the episode after it had begun, look closely at the evidence and at her interpretation, and see the flaws in her first impression. She was proving to herself that she need not be dominated by old blind "feelings."

Discovering these capabilities for Clara was like walking from the dark into daylight, though taking second looks and testing reality required her careful attention and practice. Clara was gradually learning the essentials of effective thinking. New information was entering her memory as she discovered her new-found abilities to stop, look and see with intentional choices. Learning to take stock of herself and choose more effective behavior gave Clara new confidence. In the process, her disturbing fears and wariness were intruding less into her life.

Ken, too, was involved in new experiences. Although he could acknowledge his own straying tendencies, he discovered that his "fun" had had insufficient substance to warrant its cost. With Clara's morose suspicions and moods subsiding, he was finding real fun with her and the children. Picnics in the park, attending church together, visiting other young couples, planting a garden, and redecorating the house were pleasures they were discovering together. Ken was beginning to grow up.

Was Clara cured? People can be cured of pneumonia if the infecting organism is subdued to the point that bodily defenses can effectively take over. The same is true with persistent personal problems, except for one crucial difference. Our immune system automatically protects our bodies. We have to *intentionally* protect our minds. To the extent that Clara continues to utilize her self-protective capabilities, she is cured of the ravages of her "misinformation virus."

The next two chapters will consider basic mental processes that are of vital importance in our lives. They are the sources of our unique powers and also of our unique problems.

CHAPTER 3

Our Two Worlds

Unlike animals that struggle solely with vicissitudes of the external environment, we humans are in double jeopardy. Not only must we contend with our environmental world, but also the world represented in our minds.

Our mental world is like a hall of mirrors with images from different phases of our entire lives reflecting from the past onto information coming in from the present.

Clara's experiences, related in the preceding chapter, illustrate our double jeopardy: how insecurities imbedded in ourselves produce interpretations that compound difficulties in our circumstances.

In this chapter, we will look briefly at our primary mental processes and how they relate to each other.

Primary Mental Processes – The Information Synthesizers

Senses (S)

All the information stored in our memories got there

through our sensory systems – the sensory organs and sensory nerves that relay messages to our brains from the environment and our bodies.

Sense organs automatically convert physical energies and chemical stimulation into nerve impulses. Sensory nerves transmit these impulses to our brains where they are instantly interpreted by perception. Both the sensory images and interpretations are retained in memory very briefly or longer, depending on their significance and associations with other information in memory.

What we do with input from our senses depends upon what it means to us, how it is interpreted by perception and thought. While our interpretations can be out in left field, our senses seldom mislead us, assuming they are not diseased, defective or worn out.

Memory (M)

Memory is the heart of our mental world and of all that distinguishes us as individuals. If it were obliterated, we would be little more than meat and bones. It is the bedrock of our learning potential, a time bridge that links information retained moment by moment. From infancy to the present, our memories are the "eyes" in our heads with which we can look into our minds.

Our memories have been accumulating information all our lives. This accumulation creates a panorama of life, unique for each of us, that is laced with meanings of every sort – joy, sorrow, success, failure, hope and frustration. All of our accomplishments and even the thousands of tasks we take for granted – like opening doors, reading books, communicating with language, buttoning shirts – depend upon the continual flow of information provided by our memories.

Information we recall is represented in the form of language and a variety of sensory images, such as memories of sights, sounds or other sensations. We also remember "feelings" such as love, joy, fear and despair.

Memory <u>retains</u> information, and through recall <u>releases</u> it. Both retention and recall can occur <u>automatically</u>. Although we can intentionally choose to recall any information available from memory, we cannot retain information by merely choosing to remember it. Several other conditions are necessary for that.

Sensory input is not the only source of information stored in memory. Memory also retains information generated by our perceptions and thoughts. We can only know how we perceive and what we think through recall from memory.

Perception (P)

Perception is like a computer that scans memory's vast network of information at incredible speed and instantly interprets sensory input. Some sensations, such as pain, have inborn meanings, but most sights, sounds, smells and other sensory sensations mean nothing until they are interpreted by our perceptions. If we see a dog with a frothing mouth stumbling toward us, the visual sensations themselves neither hurt us, please us, nor shed light on the significance of the scene. Add to this, however, information from memory about rabid dogs and we instantly perceive danger.

Our survival depends on being able to quickly identify and discriminate, to anticipate consequences and, spontaneously or intentionally, to select behaviors that are likely to be effective. In order to develop appropriate responses to an unlimited set of conditions, we begin developing perceptions of our physical environments, our social environments and our subjective selves very early in life.

Perceptions continually affect not only our emotional reactions and behavior, but also subtly influence beliefs and the strength of memories. *Most important, perceptual interpretations and anticipations record on memory.* Because of this, it is within our power to recall them and become aware of the meanings they create.

Thought (T)

Thinking is action without muscle. It is operating with representations of tangible things and intangible concepts. We think with information from memory that is retained in various forms, e.g., sensory memories, images, language. When we think about something that just happened, we are thinking about what we remembered.

Thought occurs in two different ways. We can <u>intentionally</u> choose to think and we think <u>automatically</u>.

In either case, thought is <u>motivated</u>. An important form of motivation is lack of information we need or want. We consciously focus attention on thinking because we are curious, need to resolve problems, make decisions, develop plans or gain understanding.

Worrisome thought is likewise motivated by uncertainties (not knowing what we need to know). Our human brains are especially disposed to go off on their own and think for us when we do not understand our problems or know what to do about them. These thoughts, though unintentional, still motivate much of our behavior by the importance they attribute to situations and the decisions and choices they make.

The importance we attach to any information good or bad and the frequency with which we dwell on it influence how strongly it is established in memory. Automatic brooding and mulling over personal uncertainties are both bad thinking and bad for us. Such worry generates more worry. As these vicious cycles repeat themselves *ad infinitum*, not only do uncertainties, threatening notions and doubts grow in importance, but they also gain strength in memory.

The good news is that, *like our perceptions, thought records in memory.* Hence, we are able to recall our thoughts, evaluate them and, by choice, become acquainted with the beneficial and destructive powers of this uniquely human capability. Memories can be changed; perceptions can be changed; thoughts can be changed; and vicious circles perpetuated by these processes can be eliminated!

The figure graphically illustrates how senses, memory, perception and thought relate one to the other. These integrated information processing capabilities are the fundamental "workhorses" of our new brains.

Information that originates in the

20

environment and our bodies is taken in by sensory organs (S) and relayed to our brains by sensory nerves. There it is instantly interpreted by perception (P) and stored in memory (M). Memory feeds old and new information back into perception and thought (T). Perception and thought, in turn, record back in memory.

Our two worlds consist of information in two entirely different forms: physical-tangible and representational-intangible. To exist, our mental world requires auxiliary systems. It relies on senses to take in physical-tangible information from the environment and sensory nerves to relay it to the brain. Muscles, supportive structures, and motor nerves make actions possible. Actions get us about in our external world, enable us to communicate and orient our senses for obtaining information. If we were incapable of action, our mental world would be a veritable Sahara. Arousal processes maintain physiological balance and energize emotions, creating sensations that contribute to a rich tapestry of feelings. Without the interaction of all these systems, we could hardly have a mind at all. Our minds are a composite of the mental (cognitive) processes just discussed and these auxiliary systems.

FIVE SYSTEMS OF MIND

① INPUT SYSTEMS
External Environment
Internal Environment (bodily states)

② SENSORY SYSTEMS

③ COGNITIVE
SYSTEMS
(M) Memory
(P) Perception
(T) Thought

④ AROUSAL -
EMOTIONAL
SYSTEMS

⑤ ACTION
SYSTEMS

21

The four powerful capabilities that we control directly are described in the next chapter. With these capabilities we can obtain any available information from our environment. Equally important, these are the capabilities that enable us to obtain information from our own brains – information from memory's huge store and information our brains generate. If we wish to understand our feelings, motives and behavior, we need be aware of events and conditions in our environment, our bodily states and how our minds interpret them.

CHAPTER 4

*W*indows in Our Mental World

Can we make choices? Do we have a will? Choice and will are topics that have invited thought over the ages from the ancient Greek and oriental philosophers to those in our own century. Such issues are quite important, for if we were unable to decide and choose, who would be in charge?

It is not surprising that amidst all the thoughts on choice and will, there are many conflicting viewpoints. Religions differ widely in their beliefs about our freedom to make choices. Gautama Buddha taught that our destinies in the physical and spiritual worlds hinge on how we think and choose. Many other faiths believe that our destiny is decided by the Will of God or by predestination. Theologians found it necessary to rule in favor of free choice in order to hold sinners responsible for their sins.

Freudian psychoanalytic theory contends that "unconscious" motivation is the real power in human affairs and therefore intentional choices are superficial. Pavlov's discoveries and research on conditioning captivated American psychologists in the early 1900s, giving rise to behaviorism. Staunch behaviorists believe that uncon-ditioned and conditioned stimuli evoke responses, precluding the need for intervening mental activities such as choice or will.

Who is right? In light of the galaxy of beliefs and defini-tions, it seems unlikely that the authorities will ever reach consen-sus. But, if we find from our own experiences that it works best when we capitalize on our abilities and take responsibility for our own lives, then consensus among the authorities seems irrelevant.

Choice is a mental activity that implies the chance, right or power to choose among alternatives, generally through free exercise of judgment. Willing and choosing are close relatives. We cannot will without choosing what to will and both require making deci-sions.

Choosing and deciding are motivated. We are motivated to select options that are perceived as more satisfying than others or that are perceived as less distressful. Of course, important choices are seldom that simple. Many conditions influence choices, such as knowledge of the options, amount of effort involved, personal beliefs and values, the opinions of others and self-confidence.

Choices and decisions are especially difficult when conflicts pull in different directions. Such is the case when we believe we are damned if we make a certain choice and damned if we don't. We also get stuck on the horns of dilemmas when different options seem equally important. Since nearly everything we do requires decisions and choices, deeply ingrained conflicts are crippling and contribute in many ways to perpetuating personal problems.

From our own experiences we find that, through a typical day, most of our choices are established habits that maintain the entrenched patterns of our lifestyles. Most of these occur semi-automatically, as for example, when we glance at the clock and decide it is time to leave for work. In our protected environments, our choices are made largely from among familiar things and activities.

In the natural world and unfamiliar settings, however, there are unpredictable opportunities and dangers that can make choices a matter of life and death. Under such conditions, four basic capabilities are mandatory in order to implement survival:

(1) It must be possible to rapidly obtain information from the surroundings at any time.

(2) There must be means for instantly recognizing the significance and implications of such information.

(3) A central information processor must be able to integrate such information and select responses that are appropriate for the circumstances.

(4) There must be the capabilities for executing and directing the activities selected.

The capabilities that serve these essential purposes are attention, recall, thought and action. Since they are vital for survival, they are innate, inborn capacities in humans and in all higher animals. These capabilities are wired up to operate automatically and instantaneously in coordination with each other.

Humans, however, are especially favored in that these abilities are also under voluntary control. This means we can use them when and how we please by exercising judgment and intentionally choosing what we do with them. Because of this, they are called our **Direct Choice Capabilities**. Moreover, these four capabilities are the only ones we have that are fully under our voluntary control.

These are the capabilities we used all our lives to seek and apply information that enabled us to learn about our environments and how to deal with them.

Because of these capabilities, we have another power that has been strangely neglected. This is the ability to look into our mind, observe and become aware of what transpires in our mental world. Most of the mental activities in our new brains that escape our awareness are spontaneous perceptions and thoughts. Since much of this activity does not necessarily attract attention, we are often not clearly aware of what we think and what meanings we give to events. But the interpretations and ideas represented by these processes are retained in memory when they are significant to us and repeated.

We are able to look in and see the information produced by our mental processes because of two conditions:

(1) Repeated thoughts and perceptions of any significance

are retained in memory.

(2) We can recall information from memory by intentional choice. In fact, since there are no sensory receptors to tap information retained in our brains, this is the only way we have access to information that our brains produce.

Our four **Direct Choice Capabilities** give us the power to obtain information by intentional choice from our external environments and our minds.

The four capabilities that we can employ at will are as follows:

1. *Attention.* We can intentionally direct and focus attention. This allows us to become aware of any information we choose that is obtainable through our senses or from memory.

2. *Recall.* The heart of our mental world is memory. Our every thought and action in the present is influenced by current sensory input and the nature of information retained in memory. Most of the moment by moment influences from memory occur spontaneously. But we also have access to any available information in its vast store by intentionally choosing to recall it.

We can bring into awareness information, knowledge and skills acquired over the course of our lives. We also are able to become aware of how we interpreted past happenings, what we anticipated, and how we thought about them. In addition, we can recall and be aware of our interpretations of a moment ago and what is continually preoccupying us. All such information from external and internal sources, from occurrences in the past and present that registered in memory, can be brought into awareness by intentional recall and focused attention.

Our senses let us know what takes place in the external environment. Our ability to intentionally recall information produced by our brains is like a window that enables us to look into our mental world and see what takes place there. If we are to understand our behavior, our feelings and ourselves, we must have information from both worlds. The significance or meaning of outside happenings comes from how they are interpreted inside.

3. *Intentional thought.* The ability to think intentionally is the master process of our **Direct Choice Capabilities**, as the

pituitary gland is the master gland of the endocrine system. Our intentional choices are made with decisions from intentional thought. By means of these decisions we choose when and how to use our other **Direct Choice Capabilities**. We can choose where to direct and focus attention; what to recall from memory; what and how to think; and what actions to take in any occasion.

When we pay attention to what and how we think and think effectively (as discussed in Chapter 9), we are turning on a power with limitless potentials. With it, we can direct the processes whereby we gain understanding and solve problems, both great and small, personal and practical.

4. *Action.* Striated muscles which enable us to move are under our voluntary control. Obviously, no species would survive that could not select actions appropriate for circumstances.

Unlimited purposes can be accomplished with our actions. Among them is the crucial function of feeding information back into the mind. With our actions we seek and obtain information, manipulate things and experiment. By such means we seek facts, verify our ideas, discover, apply and test options.

Whatever our decisions and plans, we can only gain confidence in them after they have been applied and tested. This requires action. As the following sequence suggests, it cannot be done by thought alone.

The experiences of real people best illustrate how our natural direct choice capabilities give us the power to become aware of, understand and cope with persistent personal problems. The next chapter will look into the troubled life of Steffen, an intelligent man with lots of persistent personal problems

(PPP's).* We will see how he learned to apply his direct choice
capabilties and with them uproot the processes that were perpetuating his problems.

---

* These are garden variety emotional problems which psychiatry for
over a century classified as neuroses. They do not include severe
psychiatric conditions diagnosed as psychoses, pathological personality disorders or organic mental disorders.

PPP's are not an "illness." They do not involve bizarre, crazy
delusions, hallucinations and behaviors. They are made up of
ordinary troubles, blunders and emotions that can become quite
extreme.

CHAPTER 5

Preoccupations

Obsessional Vicious Circles

Our brains, when used effectively, are problem solvers without equal. Unfortunately, their powers operate with ingenuity at both noble and nefarious ends of human affairs. On the dark side, our brains are vehicles for man's inhumanity to man and the primary source of individual psychological suffering in individuals. Capable of accumulating, inventing and incubating malignant information without our intent, our brains can tangle us in a maze of uncertainties and conflicts.

The following is a true account of one man's expanding maze. When we first met, Steffen was at the brink of disaster. Sensitive and intelligent, he endeavored to cope by means of idealistic beliefs about what was *right* and *should be*. His persistent efforts to live by his ideals produced only frustration. Self-doubt and disappointments dominated his thoughts. Strange feelings alarmed him.

Steffen's childhood was far from ideal. His father was an electrician who eased the monotony of his daily life by drinking beer and watching sports on TV until he fell asleep. He worked and, as he called it, relaxed, doing little else. He was not very accessible. His mother on the other hand, was too accessible. She was a simple, devout soul who found few things the way they should be. Steffen, the eldest with a younger sister and brother, was always a good boy whom Mother regarded as smarter than herself. From a tender age, he was the vessel into which she poured her endless stream of discontent. He believed it would be wrong to protest.

The family had a long heritage of Catholicism which Mother honored and Father ignored. The children all went to parochial school, and it was the church with its traditions that inspired Steffen. He looked up to the two priests who officiated at services as men of learning and authority.

Steffen attended Mass with his mother. For many years he did not understand the significance of the bells, processionals, incense, altar servers, stained-glass windows, crucifix, statues, candles and chants, but he found them mysterious, awesome and beautiful. These became Steffen's spiritual and aesthetic matrix.

Through grade school, Steffen was thin and wore thick glasses because of poor eyesight. While his peers taunted him continuously, his father seldom paid any attention to him. That is until Steffen turned ten and his father decided Steffen needed to become involved in sports. Although Steffen was eager to please and anxious to have his father's approval, he dreaded sports.

Steffen resolved this dilemma by implementing an old scheme of feigning sickness. To "prove" to others he was sick, he quit eating.

For over half a year Steffen tenaciously pursued this plan. His mother noted his apparent loss of appetite and nagged him without success to eat. Gradually Steffen's naturally thin frame became emaciated and his alarmed mother took him to the family physician. Finding no organic disorder, he was referred to a psychiatrist who diagnosed *anorexia nervosa* and initiated probes into Steffen's unconscious.

Steffen's father was not a violent man, but when he saw the bill he exploded and abruptly ended the youth's treatments. This was not of particular consequence to Steffen. What mattered was that his mother's alarm, his father's consternation, the trips to the doctors, and his skeletal appearance had successfully sidetracked the issue of Steffen's participation in sports. Believing he was out of danger, he began eating again.

Steffen, like other members of the human race, disliked being badgered. While he despised those who tormented him, he knew this natural reaction was anathema to his spiritual beliefs and values. His social philosophy was to turn the other cheek; his models were the good Samaritan and the priests of his church. Resentful, hateful or retaliatory thoughts that leaked into his awareness were sinful. He purged such occurrences through confession and prayer, but as time passed he longed to atone for his guilt in some tangible form. He decided to be like the priests and become a caretaker of souls.

Meanwhile at home Steffen became aware of some puzzling feelings. One day, as he listened to his mother's ranting, his eyes focused on a sharp knife lying on the kitchen counter. As he later recalled, "I suddenly felt resentful. Then I got very scared. I got up and put the knife in the very back of a drawer."

These strange feelings and behaviors began recurring not only when Steffen saw knives, but also when other pointed objects caught his attention. He was bewildered and wondered over and over, "Why do I feel this way? Why is the feeling so strong that I have to hide sharp things? Why did this start around Mother? I couldn't possibly want to harm her. I love her! I do not want to hurt anybody. I only want to help people." Steffen's confused feelings intensified.

Ultimately Steffen graduated with excellent grades from high school. He was encouraged to enter college and take computer programming because he liked math and was very accurate. He began courses at the community college and settled into a relatively calm period. The taunts and snide remarks of peers were nonexistent; he was away from home more and the frightening thoughts about sharp objects diminished though he continued to wonder about them.

After three quarters of "A" work, a friendly instructor recommended Steffen for a job which he badly needed. A large dairy with subsidiary poultry and egg interests needed a computer operator in its egg marketing section. Steffen was troubled about accepting the position because, from all he had read, egg yolks were rich in cholesterol and a menace to health. As he agonized over concerns that companies promoting egg consumption were profiteering at the expense of human welfare, the position was filled by someone else.

By this time, Steffen's father had developed liver cirrhosis and pneumonia and family finances plummeted. Steffen could no longer continue school, aggravating his mother's concerns and his own frustrations. At times he nearly panicked at the sight of sharp objects and his brother and sister, aware of this behavior, branded him a crazy weirdo.

Steffen's head was a kaleidoscope of shifting despair. He felt he needed to move out of his parents' home, but he did not know where to go, what to do. Without friends and with frightful thoughts preoccupying his mind, he felt he was losing control and might do something terrible. His tensions mounted; he wondered if he were crazy and if he should check into a mental hospital. He prayed all night and slept little.

Despite the anguish, Steffen set about looking for work and soon found a part-time job as bookkeeper for a charitable organization. At work his preoccupations became less distracting, but at other times they were relentless.

For Steffen, control over his fears lay in his ability to serve others' needs. As his preoccupations grew and his ability to control them diminished, his drive to do good deeds became overpowering. He continuously watched for ways to intervene in others' misfortunes, and for Steffen danger lurked everywhere. Steffen's ability to differentiate between real and imagined menaces was weakening. A neighbor's trash burning was misconstrued as a house fire with trapped victims, and he was humiliated when the neighbors found his perception funny.

Rescue attempts began interfering with Steffen's job. He perceived danger continuously and agonized over his responses to each crisis. He was certain he smelled gas and hounded the gas company to do site visits and tests,only to find that whatever he smelled was not leaking gas.

He insisted a local grocery store manager open cans of seafood on the shelf because he fancied they had a suspicious bulge. While each episode left him embarrassed and upset when he was proven wrong, he was nonetheless at a loss to respond differently. He knew it was not his responsibility to worry about such things, but in Steffen's mind failure to act would reflect a wanton disregard for the welfare of others. Disappointing outcomes, instead of warning him to more carefully consider what he was doing, were interpreted as signs that he was not trying hard enough.

The climax occurred when Steffen's grandmother needed to be moved to a nursing home. Steffen was convinced that the diuretics she was taking for high blood pressure were causing her increasing listlessness. As his grandmother grew steadily weaker, he agonized over the need to confront her doctor with this information. When he finally decided to do so, he learned the physician was on vacation in Europe. A few days later, his grandmother quietly died. Over and over Steffen was haunted by the thought that his inaction had killed his grandmother. Guilt dominated his thoughts and his inner turmoil became unbearable. The fears of sharp objects, his ineffective rescue missions and thoughts of having caused his grandmother's death compounded his tensions and despair. He slept little and was always exhausted.

Steffen confided in a priest who tried to reassure and comfort him. He advised Steffen to obtain psychological help and, though reluctant, Steffen finally agreed. This is when I first met Steffen.

Though physically frail, Steffen struck me as clearly intelligent and surprisingly pleasant despite his suffering. He was bewildered by his difficulties but genuinely intent on doing whatever he could to extricate himself from them. He often expressed himself in terms inspired by his strong religious orientation, saying things like "My body and mind are the temple of the Lord and I must get them in order."

Steffen wanted to make sense out of what was happening to him. With his interest in computers, he immediately drew an analogy between the capabilities of computers and his own abilities to deal with the information we had discussed.

One day he commented, "It's strange I never considered what I can do just by choosing. Like a super computer, if I push the right buttons I can call up information. In the same way, I can focus attention on my senses and put whatever information I want onto my *awareness screen*. I can obtain information from my memory bank, sort it, and put it into logical forms that help me draw conclusions and find solutions to problems. I can do even more than computers, because I have the ability to go places, experiment and test ideas in different situations."

For Steffen, the analogy was like magic. The realization that his act of thinking and choosing could make positive things happen unleashed a world of new possibilities for him. Fascinated, he did a lot of experimental observing by recalling troubling memories and thoughts and bringing them to his *awareness screen*. Looking at them this way, he could describe new ideas clearly and objectively. He could then recognize how flawed some of his thinking processes had been. But, in spite of the new understanding, Steffen's old thoughts and urges nevertheless persisted spontaneously.

Steffen's problems were too deeply implanted to be quickly swept away. Teased, mocked and generally harassed throughout childhood, he had no refuge in a home with a disapproving father and a complaining mother. His natural frustrations stirred a deep anger in Steffen that in turn stirred up self-condemning, guilty thoughts.

Steffen could think effectively about academic topics, but his personal difficulties were perpetuated by spontaneous bad thinking. When a problem bewildered him, he blindly groped for explanations instead of using his good reasoning abilities to reevaluate childhood notions. Sweeping generalizations, such as assuming responsibility for his grandmother's death, would fire up emotional reactions that obstructed his ability to examine the facts. His rescue missions were strongly motivated by his blind belief that his worth and salvation depended upon them.

Steffen and I took many guided tours through his memory, examining troubling episodes – external events, internal beliefs and the bases of his interpretations.

"What is most important to you?" I asked.

"For me," he said, "to be right in the eyes of God."

"And after that?" I inquired.

""I want to feel I'm okay; that I'm useful and respected."

This was not new, but the focus was sharpening.

"How could you feel most right with God?"

Steffen reiterated his beliefs that to him the ideal was doing like the good Samaritan and the priests, turning the other cheek and loving his neighbors and parents.

"How then," I asked, "are you falling short?"

Steffen's eyes reddened, his lip quivered. After a moment he sighed, "I've been deceiving myself. I don't love people like I should. I'm not really a good Samaritan. I'm a nobody, a stupid failure," he sobbed.

Steffen was ready to lift the veil and reexamine his beliefs and their effects. We talked about disliking in the most basic, natural terms. It could not be denied that we naturally dislike physical pain. "Don't we also dislike psychological pain," I asked, "such as being belittled, humiliated and disappointed?"

"Of course, nobody likes that sort of thing," Steffen acknowledged. Looking back over some of his troubling episodes and how he really had felt under such conditions, he could not deny that such experiences had been extremely disturbing. With more observations, he abandoned his righteous defense and confessed that, in fact, he had felt hatred for people who kept causing him pain.

With some intelligent thought about natural life and Divine purposes, he eventually concluded that God must have intended that living things should struggle to survive. Taking this idea further, Steffen decided that survival does require protecting oneself and that the ability to dislike is a natural spur to protect oneself from pain and harm.

Steffen thought a great deal about these matters, recalling and observing his own experiences, testing and experimenting with new ideas about them. He conceded that it was natural for him to dislike schoolmates who had harassed him. He looked more closely at his feelings toward his mother and acknowledged that he had disliked her nonstop complaining but had never felt he could protest. He recalled the frustration he had felt in wanting to shut her up and then remembered that the first time he had registered a fear of sharp things was on such an occasion.

Next Steffen examined his relationship with his father, finally admitting his father was alcoholic and self-absorbed. For the first time he could see that what he had assumed was his father's lack of caring for him was really an inability to care for anyone. And he began to see how the way he interpreted his father's behavior contributed to his notions of worthlessness and how a hidden dislike for his father caused guilty thoughts over breaking the Fifth Commandment.

Understandably, Steffen harbored resentments, but he disguised them without being aware of it. Whenever such bitterness leaked into his awareness, his thoughts automatically generated anxiety and guilt. At first he sought expiation in prayer, but later such feelings and a need to prove his worth became driving forces behind his rescue missions. As efforts to atone for his guilt repeatedly proved ineffectual, self-doubts deepened and needs to prove his worth intensified. These dilemmas led to nightmarish preoccupations and constant quandaries. In short, he was caught in a maelstrom of vicious circles.

What could be changed? Principles? Beliefs? Self-attitudes? Perceptions and thoughts? Behavior? Environmental conditions? All of these could be changed. Steffen was changing his notions about disliking and anger, and a more realistic belief was confirmed by conversations with his priest who assured him such natural feelings were not sinful.

Changing beliefs reduced the incentive to rescue others. Less intensely driven, he was better able to stop, carefully reconsider and make intentional, reasoned decisions instead of being driven by blind impulses. Steffen's deeply religious and humanistic principles did not need changing, but they did need tempering. Most important, he needed to begin experiencing himself as a real person in a real world with capabilities that could be valuable to others and to himself.

His church had several philanthropic programs, such as aid for the elderly, tutoring school children, food and clothing banks, and several hospital programs. We considered how participation in these could enable him to associate with other caring individuals and provide tangible help for people in need. Steffen was incredulous that these ideas had never occurred to him. "My crazy ideas," he said, "had me trying to be like Jesus Christ instead of doing real things with real people."

Steffen was enthusiastic about these new approaches. He decided to tutor and made arrangements to do so, realizing that he was proving his caring for others by his actions.

It took nearly six months to get to this point, but with these issues focusing and new skills developing, other changes came more easily. Steffen had learned to identify what he believed and thought, and how blind beliefs had influenced his interpretations and these, in turn, had motivated his self-defeating behavior. As he dealt more effectively with inner problems, he was able to turn more attention to external ones.

Living in his parents' home was a drab arrangement that offered little in the way of stimulation or enlightenment. This situation was made worse by his lack of friends and social outlets. As his personal troubles mounted, he became more isolated and had too much time for despairing preoccupations. Steffen clearly realized how unhealthy his lack of involvement had been and he was ready to apply his talents to becoming a productive participant in life.

While exploring his interests and aspirations, several options emerged that could be readily translated into action. He decided to take advantage of a bargain health program at the local YMCA.

As ideas and new possibilities lined Steffen's landscape, he also talked about a fascination for birds that had begun in childhood and decided to join the Audubon Society.

Another topic that emerged unexpectedly was an interest in hypnotism. I had shown him the rudiments of Zen meditation, which at times had helped disrupt his preoccupations. We felt it might be a useful self-quieting technique for him to learn some skills in self-hypnosis. This led to signing up for a hypnotism class at the community college.

As Steffen became involved in all of these new activities, he found that he was not only absorbing and storing in memory new information, but also making contacts with other people. Before long, he met a girl in his class and discovered that some feelings could be beautiful.

Adding to these ventures, a CPA he met hired Steffen to assist him. The additional income enabled Steffen to take a course that put him back on track in his explorations of the computer field.

Steffen had automatically thought and acted like a robot for years. A sensitive social being, Steffen continually suffered from the belief that he was an unvalued outcast. His memory had been an album of disparagement, filled with schoolmates' belittlement, his father's repudiation, siblings' scoffing and mother's laments. Self-esteem was the natural victim of such implants. Humanistic ideals were his only hope. He clung to the belief that he would be valued for his good works. But with efforts blindly motivated by desperate needs to salvage self-worth, failures and frustrations were the inevitable consequences.

Finally, mounting desperation motivated Steffen to explore, with an appropriate guide, uncharted territories of his life. There he began to discover unfamiliar domains of his mind, emotions, behavior and their consequences. As he gained new facts with which to think, intelligent choices could be made that began producing rewarding outcomes.

With less mulling to incubate them, Steffen's emotions, moods, fear, guilt, depression, bodily tensions, sleeplessness and other symptoms subsided. Reduced mental and emotional clutter freed his intelligence to address real life matters, such as education, employment, independent living, pursuing interests and enjoyment, companionship and even romance.

Steffen worked diligently with many ups and downs, but within the short space of one year was on an entirely different path. When I saw him four years later, despite some disappointments and setbacks, neither inner nor outer difficulties had been able to reestablish his self-perpetuating vicious circles.

CHAPTER 6

*A*utomatic Thought
Benign & Malignant

We humans constantly think, even while sleeping. Most of this continual thought is automatic. Our brains are continually active recalling, rehearsing, keeping track of where we are and where we are going, hashing over problems and groping for answers.

Thinking is like breathing. It can be automatic or intentional and we can partially control it. For example, we can voluntarily choose to stop breathing for a little while or alter our breathing patterns. When we stop paying attention to breathing, it resumes automatically. Similarly, we can intentionally choose how and what we think. But when we are not deliberately thinking or concentrating on something, thinking goes on by itself, to our benefit or detriment.

Benign Automatic Thought

Under familiar circumstances, we act and think spontaneously in accord with habits developed over the course of our lives. It is efficient and comfortable to operate spontaneously with no more attention or deliberation than is necessary. Benign automatic thought keeps us oriented and coordinates information from senses and memory with ongoing events and behavior.

Such spontaneous mental activity serves many essential purposes. It keeps us oriented as to who and where we are in time and place, distinguishes sensory input from the billions of bits of information already in memory, and keeps us in touch with what we have done and what needs doing.

Myths have developed around the claim that problems can be solved by automatic "subconscious thought." Renowned people such as Steinmetz and Brahms described how solutions to difficult problems suddenly and effortlessly occurred to them. It is important to note, however, that prior to such remarkable occurrences, they had devoted extensive effort to assembling information and exploring countless options, all of which were retained in memory. We might like to believe that our brains will solve our problems effortlessly, but automatic thought never solves problems unless memory already contains the information necessary to form solutions.

Malignant Automatic Thought

In addition to its organizing and coordinating roles, automatic thought surges in response to perceived dangers and uncertainties. Such mental activity is one of many inborn safety features essential for implementing self-protection and survival. It is a monitoring process that maintains vigilance and keeps us reminded of important matters needing attention.

When confronted with distressful uncertainties, we are prone to automatically worry about them. Examples of this natural tendency abound in everyday life. We may worry about running out of gas before reaching the next gas station. We worry about unpaid bills. We usually find this very disagreeable, but are ultimately thankful if our worries nagged us into taking care of problems needing attention.

Nevertheless, the beholder's perception decides what is threatening and dangerous. Whatever we believe is threatening, be it real or fantasy, sets automatic thought in motion. Activated by phantoms, automatic thought flips 180° from protector to malignant menacer.

All normal human brains are subject to floundering in semi-conscious automatic thought to various degrees. With our unique abilities to represent information symbolically, we also are uniquely susceptible to acquiring and believing misinformation. Floundering in automatic thought saturated with misinformation is a uniquely human vulnerability that can happen to the best of people.

When driven by fear, frustration or despair, malignant automatic thought can grow into cyclones that blow away our ability to think effectively. As it cycles, it keeps difficulties vividly in memory, anticipates problems that do not exist, balloons the importance of difficulties, elevates bodily tensions and generates disturbing symptoms such as anxiety and depression. Unchecked malignant thought can gain momentum and shut out intelligent choices until we are left to the wiles of its ungoverned rampages.

When such thoughts are rampaging, we feel disturbed. The feelings attract attention, but they are only the fin of the shark. Under the surface, malignant thought cycles in habitual patterns driven by menacing beliefs and uncertainties. Distress is compounded with elevated arousal and reduced effectiveness which are likely to be perceived as signs of physical and mental collapse. As all this swirls under the surface of clear awareness, problems remain and malignant automatic thought cycles on in vicious circles, such as the following:

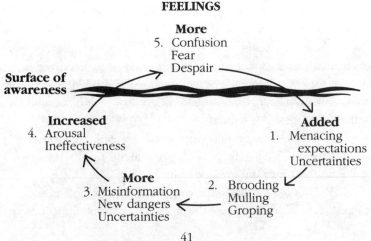

FEELINGS

More
5. Confusion
Fear
Despair

Surface of awareness

Increased
4. Arousal
Ineffectiveness

Added
1. Menacing
expectations
Uncertainties

More
3. Misinformation
New dangers
Uncertainties

2. Brooding
Mulling
Groping

41

Common patterns and consequences of malignant automatic thought

We are all alike in certain major respects: we learn, form habits and are motivated by common needs to gain and maintain satisfactions and to avoid and eliminate distresses. We encounter problems in our environments and problems within ourselves. Considering these and other ways we are alike, it is not surprising that different people experience similar patterns of malignant automatic thought that feed back and cause personal problems to persist. Following are some of the more common of these self-perpetuating patterns.

1. *Self-doubts and dread of others' opinions.* If we feel inferior, inferiority thoughts are active. Since ideas about ourselves are of primary importance, it is natural to suffer concerns about how others regard us when we seriously doubt our own worth and competence.

Self-doubters are ashamed and bewildered by the inadequacies they feel and harbor a need to hide their felt inferiority. These concerns permeate their thoughts and create a dread of being watched for fear that others will judge any shortcomings as harshly as they themselves judge them.

The common "restaurant phenomenon" illustrates this problem. Many self-doubting people express a fear of restaurants, because in such situations they believe themselves to be under constant scrutiny. Disturbing concerns like this elevate physiological arousal and, when arousal is high, nervousness and awkwardness increase the likelihood of blunders. After a few episodes in which such experiences occur, sufferers become haunted with dread of their recurrence. As they see it, such happenings are profoundly humiliating public demonstrations of their ineptitude, weakness, or mental instability.

Such miserable apprehensions are repeatedly mulled over and anticipated. Ultimately public environments may become so threatening that they are avoided entirely.

2. *Groping for explanations.* "Why?" is a favorite question inspired by troubled feelings. Unfortunately it puts the cart before

the horse since nothing can be explained until essential information has first been obtained.

Instead of asking *what* keeps recurring to make the problems persist, a common tendency is to shut off intelligence and automatically grope for explanations of puzzling feelings: "*Why* am I so anxious for no reason?" "*Why* do I feel so inferior?" "*Why* can't I ever do anything right?" "*Why* does mother love sister more than me?"

Like the pot of gold at the end of a rainbow, answers to these "whys" are never found. As the same questions are endlessly recycled, problems persist and uncertainties accumulate.

3. *Bottling-up.* Resentment and frustration never come over us without reason. Rather, they stem from festering preoccupations over having been taken advantage of and subsequent hurts and disappointments. People especially prone to such distresses shrink from protecting their interests and expressing their preferences.

Such inclinations are rooted in fears that disagreements bring retaliations, dislike and rejection. Strong beliefs of this sort motivate habitual attempts *to make the world safe by appeasing and submitting.* This behavior is then rationalized by claims of not wanting to hurt others' feelings without recognizing that the underlying fears leave one wide open to exploitation.

The disappointments accumulated by such preoccupations are not merely stored in a bottle. Instead, they actively build charges in one's head as in a condenser. Resentments and hurts incubate in thought as troubling episodes are reviewed and disappointments and frustrations are rehashed. When the charge builds to the limit of capacity, it bursts forth in an emotional binge. After such a discharge, guilt-thought takes over and the habitual patterns of appeasing and submitting are resumed in attempts to make amends.

4. *Perfectionism.* This common compensation consists of attempting *to make the world safe by being flawless.* Like "bottlers," perfectionists are unduly concerned over others' opinions of them. These concerns motivate putting considerable effort into making what they believe are faultless impressions. Whatever they do must be done "right" and beyond reproach.

43

It is a terrible strain to maintain this lifestyle. It can be equally stressful for anyone associated with it. Such people live a no-win life and impose the same on those under their jurisdiction.

There are few rewards since no matter how meticulously a job is done, it seems never to be done as well as it should be. There also is no satisfaction from praise since compliments are sabotaged. Praise is perceived as a phony attempt to make an undeserving person feel good.

Perfectionistic tendencies range from mild to severe and affect a large number of people, perhaps most of us to various degrees. The majority of us settle into our level of perfectionistic habits and tend to stay there. For many, these tendencies compound into vicious circles that ensnare them in serious persistent personal problems (PPP's). During early phases of compounding perfectionism, sufferers typically do their jobs exceptionally well, although they seldom think so. As this problem worsens, self-imposed exactitudes become increasingly burdensome until every task is arduous. Such effort, urgency and lack of anticipated satisfaction begin to conflict with the compulsion to do everything right. When demands become too burdensome, motivation shifts to seeking relief. Then an astonishing thing happens. A person known for his meticulousness goes completely "to pot" and his responsibilities become a shambles. To the amazement of everyone who knows him, he becomes an excuse-making procrastinator. At this stage depressive preoccupations begin taking over.

5. *Self-pity.* Most of us indulge in this variety of rumination when life is not going well. An accumulation of disappointments, frustrations and injustices parade around in our automatic thoughts. We struggle to maintain self-value by blaming others, circumstances, or fate for our misfortunes. At times we even enjoy our self-commiseration. However, it can get out of hand.

Spontaneously seeing ourselves as oppressed victims of a fate beyond our control fills memory with fictitious proof that we really are pitiful, helpless creatures. Such erosions of self-worth exact a heavy toll of decomposing confidence, impaired functioning and despairing feelings.

6. *Guilt-thought.* Few people recognize that feeling guilty is

a product of our own automatic thoughts. Feeling guilty is commonly believed to be a state that is imposed on us by others or somehow inflicted upon us for past wrongdoings.

Feeling guilty is explained by some theorists as an <u>unconscious</u> need to punish ourselves. "Unconscious?" Realistic self-observation will show that feeling guilty always stems from automatically wallowing in self-blame and self-condemnation. Instead of intentionally thinking about how we can right our wrongs, the old parental, social, religious edicts ("You should feel ashamed!") dominate and guilt-thought flows.

It is essential for our own and society's welfare that we have a conscience, that we have firm beliefs about right and wrong. But that does not mean the laws of God and mankind require that when there are infractions of our principles we must sink into orgies of self-condemnation.

Guilt-thought can become an habitual preoccupation that is all cost with no benefit or profit. We learn nothing and accomplish nothing from it. Easily triggered, automatic guilt-thought that ignores reality cripples. People thus inclined fail to protect themselves from others' impositions because they fear that doing so will make them feel guilty.

We all make mistakes and inadvertently, or even consciously, do things that are against our principles. When we sincerely regret what we have done, we have two obligations: 1) make amends to the extent possible, and 2) learn from our mistakes and correct our ways. In this regard, there are two kinds of mistakes we need learn from. One is that of being an exploiter of others. The second is letting our "guilt feelings" turn us into wimps for others' exploitation.

7. *Childhood memories.* During childhood, we acquire the foundations of our values, interests, beliefs, needs and related behaviors. Later in life, many of the conditions under which our attitudes and habits developed change. Nevertheless, childhood influences often persist into adulthood with little attention or awareness on our part.

We enjoy reminiscing over pleasant and amusing recollections from childhood. But we may also have painful memories that haunt us. Some troubling memories not only intrude into thought, but also blindly motivate persistent efforts to satisfy unmet childhood needs.

A very basic need for us all, social creatures that we are, is evidence that we are accepted and, hopefully, valued by others. This need was especially strong when, as children, we were primarily dependent on our family for such reassurances. If there were few or none, many painful longings can remain for the child who was adrift in a home with no affectionate moorings.

Different consequences result from these situations which are by no means always predictable. Some people with such backgrounds are able to apply adult thinking to the frustrating childhood memories that remain. They then accept the fact that no affectionate bond was or is forthcoming from their parents and decide it is fruitless to expect it. They may have the good fortune of being compensated with love in their own marriages. In contrast, there are others whose frustrating memories of their loveless homes haunt their thoughts and maintain childhood yearnings for parental love.

Preoccupations with such frustrated yearnings can induce persistent seeking without recompense. A sad picture emerges of an adult in his or her forties or fifties repeatedly turning to the same aging parent with longings for a kind word, a compliment and a token of caring. The image fades with the grown child always leaving empty handed, sadder and no wiser.

When no more birdseed is in the feeder, the birds stop coming to it. But preoccupations with childhood frustrations have a strange power to override the fundamental psychological principle that reinforcement is necessary to maintain behavior.

8. *Depressive thought.* Depression can be the most serious form of self-depreciation. When it swells into urges to exterminate oneself, depression becomes a state that overrides the most powerful motivation of all, the survival instinct.

It is impossible to struggle with the ups and downs of life without experiencing periods of discouragement. When life seems at a standstill and we are bored, it is also hard to avoid the doldrums. Poor health and physical disorders that deplete energy and vigor favor downheartedness. Losses of friends and loved ones, financial and material disappointments, and failures to achieve valued goals are especially conducive to despairing thought. We all have turns at such letdowns which we refer to as being depressed.

Some psychiatric circles regard major depression as a genetically transmitted disorder or, at least, they believe that there is an inherited proneness to this condition. This theory is in agreement with the fact that depression is more common in people from families in which forbears were said to be depressed. Nevertheless, there are still many questions about this issue. For example, there is considerable evidence that children learn beliefs, attitudes, ways of thinking and behaving from parental influences and models. It cannot be discounted that being brought up in a household with a morbidly depressed parent who year after year reiterates attitudes of worthlessness, helplessness, and hopelessness could establish similar attitudes in receptive offspring.

In any event, even if proneness to depression were a biological phenomenon transmitted by genes, it is not possible to be pathologically depressed while simultaneously occupied with hope, enthusiasm, interests, verve and a zest for life.

Although personal details differ, the common pattern of depressive thought typically includes three main features which are remarkably consistent from person to person. They amount to a depressive triad that includes: a) recurrent self-blame and self-depreciation that can become self-hate; b) preoccupation with mistakes and shortcomings that are construed as proof of being ineffectual and helpless; and c) projections into the future that leave a bleak and hopeless picture.

Under such conditions, nothing is of interest and most motivation is seriously impaired. Such loss of motivation is experienced as a lack of interests and disinclination to do anything, often to the point of spending long periods in bed. The resulting inactivity and unproductiveness is interpreted as proof of helplessness and worthlessness. Such proof feeds back into the depressive mill and, as it grinds on, life becomes increasingly unbearable. At such times the "misinformation viruses" are having a heyday replicating themselves with destructive information.

9. *Anxious thought.* Another variety of malignant, automatic thought induces and perpetuates anxiety. Anxiety is a diffuse fear state which is experienced as feeling apprehensive, nervous and tense for no clearly identifiable *external* reason. People who are anxious and "don't know why" have not learned to check out their automatic thinking.

Anxiety, like depression, is maintained by disturbing preoccupations. These, too, evolve around three main concerns: a) recurrent anticipations of disturbing things that might happen to oneself, loved ones and anything else of personal importance; b) uncertainty about when, where and how the dreadful happenings might occur; and c) dread of helplessness, of not knowing how to cope with the impending disasters.

An important aspect of feeling helpless in conjunction with both panics and anxiety is often overlooked. When these states are intense, physiological arousal is very high. It will be observed in Chapter 12 (Arousal) that we are all so constituted that our effectiveness is inversely related to arousal. Beyond a point, the more intensely we are aroused, the more our general effectiveness drops off. Anyone who has been overly aroused for long periods is naturally disposed to anticipate reduced control of both thinking and acting. Reduced control of these faculties is particularly disturbing when insecurities and self-doubts are high from prolonged anxious preoccupations.

As with depression, we cannot be anxious with a placid mind. When we are anxious, we are preoccupied with threatening anticipations and our inability to contend with them effectively. These are the fundamental conditions of fear.

Horses were born to run. We humans were born to think. Our big brains are constantly active, when not by choice, then spontaneously. Our styles of thinking were learned, mostly by indoctrination, happenstance, trial and error. School and home taught us <u>what</u> we are supposed to think, but little about how to think effectively. Early in life our ways of thinking and behaving began accumulating and developing into spontaneous habits.

Although habits become automatic, they do not spontaneously, helter-skelter turn themselves on and off. They are activated

48

by motivating conditions. We learn. We form spontaneous habits. Our habits of thought and behavior are motivated by events and what they mean to us.

We are equipped with inborn automatic processes to aid our survival, such as the immune system, arousal processes to energize vigorous action, emotions of fear and anger that orient flight and fight reactions, and the ability to form habits which become packaged patterns of spontaneous thought and action. These did not evolve to make us feel good but to aid survival.

Automatic thought is an essential aid to survival. When motivated by threatening conditions, it is a monitoring process that reminds and warns. It maintains alertness and elicits preparations for self-protective responses to tangible dangers.

Consider how we would think in an environmental situation with known dangers. We learned that rattlesnakes bite and their venom is poisonous, possibly lethal. If we were walking in grass where rattlesnakes abound, it would be virtually impossible not to think about rattlesnakes and be vigilant. At the core, such thoughts and concerns are induced by beliefs based on learned facts about rattlesnakes and the terrain. Although the thoughts and vigilance are reactions to ideas, they are adaptive since the ideas represent real dangers.

Adaptive automatic thought differs from maladaptive (malignant) automatic thought in two primary ways: 1.) Adaptive thought reminds and warns of dangers. Maladaptive thought creates them. 2.) Adaptive thought seeks information for coping with problems. Maladaptive thought cycles misinformation and precludes seeking facts that could help solve problems.

Many maladaptive beliefs can lurk in memory, such as believing oneself lacking in coping abilities, others' respect, and the capacity to manage emotions and troubling thoughts. Threatening uncertainties inherent in such beliefs keep automatic thought watchful and on guard, the same as though one were in dangerous territory. In rattlesnake country, such thought protects from real dangers. In the realm of haunting memories, automatic thought reverses its protective role and becomes malignant, creating dangers as it cycles.

It is of utmost value to recognize the fact that whatever was learned can be changed with new learning. It is amazing what we can accomplish when we understand and apply our power to make intentional choices. With them we can gain information about ourselves never seen before. With new awareness of old distorted beliefs and their adverse effects, we are ready to start work on identifying and correcting them. As such work proceeds, their dominance recedes, enabling us to master our common sense and apply it to learning new adaptive habits of thought and action.

Later chapters will chronicle the experiences of different people with different PPP patterns. These will illustrate how we can learn to turn off malignant automatic thought and take charge with the four survival capabilities that are ours to use with reasoned intentional choices. These are the capabilities that can change us from problem generators to problem solvers.

Malignant automatic thought takes on many interesting varieties. In the next chapter we will look at some of the most common types and some of their effects.

CHAPTER 7

*E*ffects of Malignant, Automatic Thought

As thinking creatures, our natural inclination when confronted with problems is to think in an effort to understand, decide and plan what to do. When, instead of effective, intentional thought, malignant automatic thought takes over, many unwanted effects develop such as the following:

1. *Effects on memory.* Repetition of important information and actions strengthens memory and establishes habits. Automatic rehashing of disadvantageous beliefs and attitudes firmly implants these ideas in memory. The more firmly material is established in memory, the longer it is retained and the more readily it can be recalled and influence interpretations. Thus, thought and memory form a feedback loop. Troubling ideas that are continually rehashed are firmly established in memory and become increasingly available to enter automatic thought and perception, which in turn maintain and strengthen the ideas in memory.

51

2. *Interference with retention.* Troubled people frequently complain that their memory has deteriorated. They even worry that their brain is damaged. This is not the case. While preoccupation strengthens retention of material dwelt on, it also interferes with retaining desired information. Our retention of any information is facilitated by three things we usually do spontaneously: (a) pay attention to what we want to remember; (b) make sure we understand it; and (c) repeat or rehearse the information. When we are preoccupied with disturbing problems, our preoccupations preclude taking these necessary steps to assure retention. Under these conditions, we find that what we want to remember simply is not available – there is too much interference for it to stick.

3. *Effects on perception.* First impression interpretations of anything we sense – our  perceptions – are based largely on associations stored in memory. The strongest memories and associations have the strongest influences on perception. Notions that are firmly implanted in memory by repetitive thought are the ones most likely to emerge as perceptual interpretations. Since perceptions themselves are retained, they too strengthen related information in memory and, as with thought, form feedback loops.

A person who perceives dogs as repulsive, dangerous creatures automatically reminds himself that dogs are repulsive and dangerous every time he sees one, and perceives it that way.

4. *Effects on the frequency and importance of troubling experiences.* Recurrent thought about troubling events, in effect, repeats the experience each time around. Thus, <u>one disappointment that</u>

is thought about a thousand times is a thousand-and-one disappointments. In a similar vein, recurrent thought about troubling experiences makes them increasingly important. One troubling experience thought about a thousand times is a thousand times more important than one such experience. To make matters worse, exaggerations and misrepresentations creep into automatic thought, as in dreams, and inflate their significance out of proportion. Since we seldom subject our automatic thought to reality testing, it is ideal for ballooning molehills into mountains.

5. *Effects on belief.* Another feature of rehashing experiences and concerns is that repetition tends to strengthen belief. This is an inductive process whereby the more times we experience a given relationship between certain events and certain interpretations, the more we are inclined to believe "that's the way it truly is." "If you tell people something often enough, they will believe it" was one of Hitler's credos. This principle operates full tilt with malignant notions and misperceptions that our heads tell us with automatic reiterations.

6. *Effects on motivation.* Perception and thought are primary sources of psychological motivation. How we "see" it sets the stage for what we are motivated to do. When we interpret a situation as dangerous, we are motivated to take protective action, whether it is really dangerous or only how we "see" it. What we do and don't do in action determines outcomes and outcomes, in turn, influence our expectations. Expecting to fail, for example, induces not trying. If we won't try, then indeed we can't succeed. When such expectations automatically block trying, the victim is locked into a self-fulfilling prophecy: the expectation is the outcome that, in turn, reinforces the expectation.

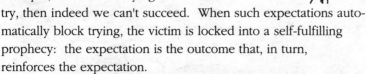

7. *Effects on emotional arousal.* Distressful preoccupation is the main psychological process that maintains arousal – the bodily reactions accompanying emotional states – at an artificially

elevated level. How long we dwell on troubling thoughts determines how long arousal will remain elevated.

Our abilities to think and act automatically, when productive, are highly valuable assets. They are like the automatic pilot of an airplane that manages innumerable details with great speed and efficiency. Not only is it efficient and beneficial to be able to think and act spontaneously, but we also like to operate this way. Fluent speech or any rapid, skilled activity would be impossible without this capacity. Routine behavior under familiar circumstances would be intolerably slow and burdensome if we had to pay close attention and deliberate everything we did.

However, when its program contains false, detrimental information which is fed into our perceptions and thoughts, our "automatic pilot" can be our worst enemy.

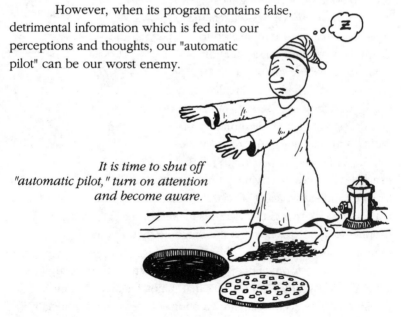

It is time to shut off "automatic pilot," turn on attention and become aware.

"Know Thyself" —
Know What Your Head Is Doing

Our memory contains the most information on earth about ourselves. This information is reflected in what and how we think. If we learn to recall and identify the issues that dominate them, our spontaneous thoughts can reveal infinitely more factual information about ourselves than could ever be gained from analyzing dreams.

Automatic thought is thus a two-way street. On one side, it provides invaluable information about ourselves. On the other side, it is a vicious circle that obscures understanding and aggravates all our other problems.

The following chapter outlines four viewpoints related to the fact that we are often not aware of what causes various "feelings" and behaviors.

CHAPTER **8**

$\mathcal{F}$our Minds
Unconscious, Black Box,
Automatic, Intentional

"All that we are is the result of what we have thought; it is
founded in our thoughts; it is made up of our thoughts." Thus
taught Gautama Buddha some 500 years before Christ. Similar ideas
have been reiterated by renowned thinkers through the ages. The
belief that thought is a powerful influence in our lives is hardly a
new idea. But what kind of thought?

Philosophical thinkers have regarded thought as the kind of
thinking we do intentionally. However, a little self observation
makes it clear that we think in two distinctly different ways. Indeed
we can choose to think <u>intentionally</u>, but we also unintentionally
think <u>automatically</u> without deciding beforehand to think. This
suggests Gautama Buddha's observations could be rephrased: All
that we are is the result of both what we have intentionally thought
and what we have automatically thought.

Our ideas about thought were further complicated by
Freud's invention of the unconscious mind. This mind interprets
and thinks, but its products remain inaccessible to awareness. The
Psychoanalytic movement that evolved from Freud's theories

attracted worldwide attention from laymen, especially those with literary interests, and influenced the theories and practice of different segments of psychiatry, clinical psychology and human service workers. The cornerstone of this viewpoint is that the unconscious mind is a prime mover in human affairs. Although mind is the main interest in Freudian theory, the significance of intentional choices and thought is relegated to the sidelines.

Conditions that until recently were called *neuroses* pose many perplexities. Among them are troubling behaviors and painful feelings that sufferers cannot account for. They ask: Why am I afraid? Why do I despair? Why do I rail at my dear mother? Such mysterious ailments and sufferers' inabilities to understand their causes were among Freud's main interests. Over many years he developed elaborate theories attributing neuroses to early childhood traumas and impulses. He accounted for unawareness of such causes by assuming that they are repressed into an unconscious mind.

Furthermore, Freud theorized that ego-threatening experiences in later life were likewise repressed or suppressed into the unconscious. Both repressed traumas of childhood and ego threats of later life were seen as fundamental causes of many different maladjustments. The puzzling lack of awareness and understanding characteristic of persistent maladjustments were likewise seen as consequences of repression into the unconscious mind. Nevertheless, the experiences thus repressed were believed to remain powerful forces that create havoc like unseen parasites.

If in fact our minds had evolved to render us unconscious of threats and traumas, then we are at a loss to account for the remarkable survival of our species.

At a later time and in academic settings not concerned with neuroses, the concept of mind was replaced with the idea of a black box into which no one could look.

By the Twenties, Experimental Psychology became absorbed in the scientific study of learned behavior. Only directly observable and measurable variables were deemed suitable for investigation. Generally, these were physical conditions and events (stimuli), physical reactions (behavior) and relations between them. Mental phenomena, such as thought, which is neither directly observable nor measurable, was regarded as an unfit topic for scientific psychology. A similar orientation permeated academic Clinical Psychology which filled journals with articles and studies on behavior maladjustment and personality measurement.

A good deal was learned about learned behavior and roles of behavior in personal problems. But the influences of thought and other mental processes were relegated to the black box.

To strict behaviorists, such as B. F. Skinner, all that we are is the result of operant conditioning, which involves the shaping and maintaining of learned behaviors through patterns of reinforcement. This conception skirts the possibility that we may intentionally assemble information from senses and memory and use it to guide deliberate choices of our actions.

Both hard core behaviorist doctrine and Freudian theories of unconscious motivation envision influences beyond our control that would render us semi-automatons. Worse, both viewpoints ignore the very capabilities that distinguish us from all other living things – our unique human abilities to shape our lives with intentional thought and conscious choices.

Unlike the strict behaviorist theories that failed to gain broad acceptance, Freud's ideas about a mysterious unconscious mind fascinated the world, a fascination that prevails in many circles to this day.

Indeed, it is true that we are creatures of habit and that most of our interpretations, emotional reactions and actions occur automatically. Likewise, we often are not aware of what causes our spontaneous feelings and behavior. But these facts in no way constitute evidence that the feelings, emotions and behaviors we do not understand are the consequences of unconscious mental processes or that conditioned responses to stimuli account for them to the exclusion of identifiable mental processes.

In contrast to Freud's assumptions about unconscious influences, a former student of his, Alfred Adler, had more practical ideas. Adler proposed that "...the unconscious is merely that part of an individual's lifestyle which he does not understand." He points out that to understand is to recognize the relationships between things. In turn, this requires paying sufficient attention to experiences occurring in our minds and environments, so that we can identify what takes place and what goes together.

This major shift in focus differs dramatically from Freud's theories. Attention, recall and thought are under our direct control. That means that if we want to, we can choose to turn our attention to sources of information both outside and inside ourselves that can enable us to understand what happens to us. In Adler's view, by our intentional choices we can become conscious of information that has eluded us from lack of attention.

We have already considered how much of our mental activitiy is automatic, and that major blind spots in our mental world are our <u>automatic perceptions</u> and <u>automatic thoughts</u>. The interpretations of these spontaneous mental processes are, to a large extent, derived from memory's great network of information and misinformation. Be they benign or malignant, automatic perceptions and thoughts do not attract attention as would a sudden loud noise. Little or no attention means little or no awareness. That is quite different from "unconscious."

When we are unaware, for lack of attention, of how we misinterpret troubling events, exaggerate their importance and perpetuate misery by brooding over them, it is small wonder that we fail to understand what is perpetuating our troubles. When we are thus ignorant of how we are deceived and misled by our own interpretations and thoughts, how can we know what needs changing? How could we learn from our experiences?

Archaeologists and paleontologists tell us that we have been around in our contemporary form for a relatively short span of time in contrast to creatures such as the scorpion and cockroach. But despite our relatively short span, we have proven ourselves a remarkably survivable species despite some of the complications our super brains can create for us.

Our survivability is attributable in part to our anatomy, to upright posture which gives us full use of our highly versatile hands. But above all in this regard is our newly evolved brain. In addition to its vast retentive, learning, and symbolic abilities, it gives us the unique capacity of consciousness – the ability to be aware of

60

and to describe ourselves and our environments and to utilize such information by intentional choice.

Our minds not only provide us with our unique conscious capabilities, but also, for better or worse, can manage most of our affairs automatically. As is true of all higher animals, activities that recur repeatedly become established habits. Our routine behavioral skills become habitual and automatic. Our perceptual interpretations and thoughts operate largely as automatic habits. This is marvelously efficient, leaving our conscious abilities available for productions more fruitful than daily routines.

What more can we ask? Our brains equip us with conscious, intentional control of essential capabilities and they also automatically manage countless routine activities. Like aircraft pilots, we can fly on automatic pilot when the going is smooth. But when trouble looms, we can turn off automatic pilot and switch to direct control. The only problem is learning how to switch off automatic mind when trouble broods and how to take over with conscious, intentional mind.

The next chapter offers some suggestions by a famous expert for improving the effectiveness of our conscious, intentional thinking.

CHAPTER 9

*T*hinking Effectively with Full Awareness

An old saw tells us, "There's more than one way to skin a cat," which is highly relevant to resolving personal problems.

The fact that there is no one-and-only right approach is supported by the recent finding of the National Institute of Mental Health that over 150 different theories and therapies are used by professionals to treat emotional disorders. Whatever our problems, we must be aware of what we are doing and engage our intelligence in seeking approaches that will best serve our needs. This being the case, sound guidelines to help sharpen our thinking are invaluable.

For this purpose, anyone can profit from the book *How We Think* by the philosopher-psychologist John Dewey. Dewey's model of good thinking goes far beyond just reasoning and logic. Throughout he emphasizes that thinking can be no better than the information with which we think.

Dewey shows that for problem solving, good thinking needs to begin with clarifying the nature of the problems we hope to solve. A clear view of what each problem consists of guides our seeking the information we need. By obtaining and organizing relevant information, the understanding we gain lets us see what changes are needed. With personal problems, memory's store of information from life's experiences (called "common sense") can provide a wealth of clues as to how we can go about making changes for the better. Finally, ideas for changes come to life only if they are applied. How well they work for us can only be determined by testing them. Good thinking requires some effort on our part. In our personal lives, no one else can do it for us.

Dewey describes the following five phases of effective thinking which are pertinent whether the subject is personal problems, buying a car, contemplating marriage or scientific research.

1. *Clearly identify each problem.*
Psychiatrists classify PPP's on the basis of symptoms. We too focus attention on symptoms when troubled and often believe they are the problem. Since symptoms are only signs of problems, that gets our thinking off to a bad start.

Therapist: "What made you decide to seek help?"

A. "I keep feeling depressed. I can't sleep. I'm losing weight. I can't control my temper and my wife wants a separation and I don't know why."

Disturbing emotions and moods, worrisome bodily sensations, troubling preoccupations, seemingly uncontrollable behaviors and a variety of occupational, social and familial conflicts and disappointments are typical symptoms of PPP's.

A problem is wanting to attain or get rid of something and not knowing how to achieve it. To start thinking effectively about PPP's, we need to identify persistent and disturbing experiences that we do not want and do not know how to eliminate or manage.

Disturbing experiences can be observed by means of our two basic sources of information: senses and memory. Instead of groping for explanations with "whys," we must learn to ask ourselves *what* disturbing experiences inside and outside keep recurring that are not being dealt with. We need to make the <u>main</u> trouble areas specific. Typically, troubled people bewilder themselves with a hodgepodge of distresses. To begin understanding problems, we must first identify a manageable number of the most troubling areas, say three or four.

2. *Seek and obtain facts.* Although most sufferers profess they do not know why they have their symptoms and problems, they nevertheless feel compelled to try to explain them. To think effectively about a problem, it is necessary to distinguish trying to explain it from observing and describing what it involves.

OBSERVE

OUTSIDE   INSIDE

Identifying facts about ourselves can be tricky. A strong force, called ego, opposes seeing ourselves as we really are. Countless people suffer throughout life evading facts rather than acknowledging correctable imperfections. They believe imperfections are reprehensible weaknesses that destroy self-worth and must be hidden.

It is said that we cannot see ourselves as others do. While others' judgments may be flawed and blind belief in others' opinions can be a serious problem in itself, we need to listen when those close to us tell us how our behavior alarms or offends them. There is a vast difference between others' analyses of our personalities and their expressions of what they personally dislike.

Anything that we dislike and cannot handle can be considered a problem. When a problem episode is in process, <u>troubling feelings</u> occur. These are important <u>signals</u> that can alert us to pay attention to what is happening inside and outside ourselves. We can note the <u>circumstances</u> and identify events that triggered difficulties. Then we can quickly recall from memory <u>how we are interpreting the situation</u> (information typically left out of the picture). In the course we need to take note of our own and

65

others' <u>behavior</u>. And to learn something from troubling experiences, <u>consequences</u> of our actions and reactions need to be considered. Many facts about PPP's are personal facts available only to us. Attention tuned to eyes and ears and recall from memory open the windows through which we can look and see what is happening inside and outside. Good thinking is well under way when we begin gathering such information.

3. *Organize the facts; find what goes together.* We are complex beings and our problems are complex. PPP's never persist because of a single cause. At the very least, our well-being is influenced by all five of the following major life areas: our external environment; our social relations; our emotional states and health; our behavior, skills and habits; and the kinds of information stored in our memories and how our mental skills and habits use this information.

PUT THINGS TOGETHER

All these major life areas influence each other in an interweaving fashion. How we interpret and think influences our behavior. How we behave influences environmental conditions, like social relations, job, income. Environmental conditions, in turn, affect our satisfactions and distresses which certainly influence our thoughts, motives and behaviors. Our body states and emotions, in turn, are markedly affected by environmental and social conditions and how we interpret and think about them.

PPP's are always unresolved, interlocking problems in several areas of life. Such problems are not problems in childhood. They are problems in the here and now. They are what is perpetuating the really important distresses and frustrations. PPP's operate in accord with the domino principle: one domino topples the next, it the next, and so on. To understand what perpetuates such vicious circles, we need to seek information about relationships, about what goes together, about how our interpretations, feelings, behaviors and their consequences affect each other.

For example, a young man suffering social isolation observed how his thinking and behavior were spoiling his social life. "My poor social life affects my thinking because I think nobody likes me. That thinking influences my behavior, so I avoid people. Naturally, I can't develop any friendships, thinking and behaving that way." Unraveling the secrets of our own vicious circles can become quite intriguing – even more so than poking around in childhood traumas.

4. *Ideas for changes come with growing awareness.* As we observe our own actual experiences in both our environmental and mental worlds and identify problems in the different major life areas, we begin seeing things we can do to make changes for the better. Because PPP's include well established environmental problems, as well as strongly motivated mental and behavioral habits, there are no quick solutions. There are, however, limitless options when we start providing our brains with information needed for effective thinking.

LET IDEAS
TURN ON

Changes can be made to alleviate problems in nearly any major life area. Some can occur more readily than others. Once firm decisions are achieved, environmental changes may be accomplished relatively quickly. Detrimental habits of perception, thought and behavior were learned, practiced and strengthened usually over many years. They cannot be changed by mere decisions and will power. New beneficial habits have to be learned to replace them. That requires, above all, persistence and practice. However, it takes only a fraction of the time to develop effective new habits that it took to establish those that were self-defeating. Negative feedback loops sustained the faulty habits. Beneficial habits grow rapidly with the positive feedback of rewarding consequences of which there are two kinds:

(1) increased competence, and (2) reduced distress.

5. *Apply and test.* How well are our beliefs, interpretations and the things we do serving us? Are they providing enduring satisfactions and reducing suffering in our lives? Any that are working in reverse clearly need changing. As we form our ideas about changes for the better, we need to verify them. They may be very logical and make good sense, but do they really add to our satisfactions and reduce our distresses? We cannot know how well changes work until they are applied and tested in trouble areas. Changes that work need to be nurtured. Those that do not need to be eliminated. This is the principle of learning from experience.

In the next chapter we will look more specifically at how two people used the five phases of effective thinking to facilitate their survival instincts, to increase enduring satisfactions and to reduce avoidable distresses. The crucial roles of good thinking for coming to grips with different kinds of problems will be seen in all the chapters describing actual experiences of troubled people.

CHAPTER 10

*G*ood Thinking about Personal Problems

Problems? What can we do? Common sense tells us to investigate the situation, get the facts, see what is happening and look before we leap. With environmental, physical, materialistic problems, we often know where to begin. If the car does not run, for example, we either investigate, discover the difficulty and fix it or find someone who can.

PPP sufferers often do not know where or how to begin getting facts or how to distinguish between interpretations and facts. Considering this dilemma, they often turn for help to others who are delighted to provide explanations and advice. Sometimes it is helpful. More often it is misleading.

Expert assistance with PPP's is much harder to find than expert assistance with the car. Regardless of whether a therapist is involved, in the final analysis it is the sufferer alone who has access to the essential facts in all major life areas. Hopefully, the preceding chapters have shed some light on how and where all of us can observe, obtain facts, put them together and think more effectively about our personal lives.

The following accounts are about how two people with very different problems used effective thinking to deal with their personal difficulties. Both Ralph and Thelma went through a similar process – Ralph by himself, Thelma with a bit of help.

I saw Ralph in conjunction with some occupational problems. In the course of describing his background, he revealed a most unusual series of childhood experiences which had left an indelible imprint.

When Ralph was three, his parents divorced. Two years later his father married a woman in her late forties who had had her fill of child rearing. Because of the marriage, which she wanted, she had acquired a stepson – the least of her desires. In order to eliminate the conflict, she hatched a bizarre plan to drown the boy.

She attempted to carry out her intentions on three occasions – twice in the bathtub and once in her washtub. Each time, Ralph's screams attracted the attention of the stepmother's older daughter who successfully intervened. Once the father discovered what she was up to, he divorced the woman, ending further episodes of this sort for young Ralph.

Nevertheless, the attempts firmly implanted terrifying associations in Ralph's memory. He had clear pictures in his head of being overpowered – helpless, pushed under water, struggling for air. These powerful memories zoomed into his perceptions and flooded his thoughts whenever his father wanted him to bathe. Ralph carried on so hysterically that his father gave up trying and allowed Ralph to sponge bathe from then on.

The intense fear persisted and generalized to a phobia about submersion in any water. He adjusted to his fears by staying out of tubs, pools and any body of water, thereby learning to manage certain emotions by avoiding dreaded situations.

When Ralph married, his wife could not understand how a big man could be afraid of bathtubs and she delighted in teasing him. Ralph was quite sensitive about these "irrational fears" and reacted to his wife's taunts with embarrassment and squabbles.

This new distress made Ralph acknowledge that his fears would not evaporate by evading them. He made a decision to address them and began the process of effective thinking by: *clearly identifying and acknowledging the problem.*

Since it is essential for survival to remember experiences that have truly threatened our lives, real traumas are not repressed. Ralph had not forgotten his terrible stepmother and he readily recalled memories he had intentionally avoided thinking about for years. They were chaotic sensory memories of being squeezed by the neck, of squirming, lunging, gasping, choking. Recollecting them, he felt raw terror, but he had yet to clearly associate these memories with his present fear of water. He thought to himself, "Here I am twenty-eight years old and when I think about that stuff, I feel real scared, like I was a little kid."

By *seeking and obtaining facts* from memory, Ralph was motivated to experiment and observe his reactions in the present. He decided to fill the bathtub, get in and pay close attention to what he really felt, an experience he had avoided for twenty-three years. When Ralph stepped in, the same fear swept over him that he had felt while looking into his memories and the connection between childhood traumas and adult fears became clear.

Because Ralph had firmly decided to face his problem, it was not difficult to gather facts from the past and present. Now fully aware, he began to *organize the facts and see how they fit together.* In his words, "That damned crazy woman kept trying to drown me. I was only five and scared to death. My instinct was to stay away from any place where anything like that could happen to me. But that didn't make the fear go away."

Ralph had no difficulty *getting ideas for changes.* "If I'm going to get over this," he reasoned, "I've got to get it into my head that everything is different now. I'm not a five-year-old kid. I'm a grown man and couldn't possibly be overpowered by such a freak. I can protect myself. I'm safe!"

He decided it was not enough simply to tell himself he was safe. He needed to keep proving it by doing, not just thinking. He therefore planned to take a bath every day "until I get those fearful memories back where they belong – twenty-three years ago."

With this understanding, determination and plan, Ralph proceeded to *apply and test his ideas.* He repeatedly demonstrated

71

to himself that by selecting his own thoughts and actions he, not childhood memories, was in control. Within two months, his apprehensions were negligible.

It is noteworthy that Ralph accomplished all this on his own with no help other than his wife's taunts. With regard to those, he said, "She made me feel like a sap and that made me determined to do something about it."

Fears of specific situations, as in the case of Ralph, can usually be endured as long as the situations can be avoided. When fears, discouragements, arousal and other symptoms are strong and groping for explanations compounds bewilderment, it is desirable to seek competent professional assistance. The best help is that which equips us to learn how to use our own natural capabilities effectively rather than that which endlessly rummages in childhood traumas, focuses on "getting feelings out" with no idea of how they are perpetuated, or concentrates on "feel good" techniques.

Thelma's problems were much more complex than Ralph's prolonged phobia. She had come from a stable, middle-class home where "old fashioned" values prevailed. Her memory was well implanted with the fundamentalist doctrine that a woman's place was that of wife, mother and homemaker, and a man's was that of head of the household.

As a wife and homemaker, Thelma began experiencing frequent, long- lasting spells of anxiety and depression. There were few satisfactions in her life and nothing inspiring to look forward to in her future. As she felt increasingly more miserable, she decided she had to do something and sought help.

At the outset, Thelma was convinced that her fears and depression were the problems. It did not take long to convince her that those were symptoms of something unwanted that was happening in her life. We needed to look more closely at recurrent troubling episodes to learn what was keeping her fearful and despairing.

We looked briefly into highlights of her background, then we turned to the present. From her descriptions, three consistent features of her life that suggested trouble emerged: 1) housekeeping had become exceedingly compelling and time consuming; 2) she felt totally dominated by and subservient to her husband; (3)

life was intolerably boring and empty. This was useful information that at least tentatively *identified problem areas.*

With some ideas about where to direct attention, Thelma began *observing, gathering and describing information* in the areas she had emphasized. She described her husband, Al, as a plodding type. He worked regularly, kept up the yard, watched sports on TV and drank a little beer most nights. He was bossy and wanted Thelma to keep a neat, clean house. If he was not satisfied, he would grumble and complain, but was never physically abusive.

Thelma also observed herself. "I've really sunk into a rut," she said. "I didn't realize it, but over the years I began putting more and more effort into trying to keep the house perfect. We have seldom gone out or done anything. I have filled the time with house cleaning. I feel as if I have been losing my mind. It has gotten so that wherever I look – window sills, baseboards, tables or chest tops – everything seems to be covered with fuzz."

While looking at distressful features, we also turned attention to what she liked, her interests. "What I wanted most," she said, "was to have children, but we haven't been able to. I suggested adopting a child, but Al would have nothing to do with that idea.

"I was a good student," Thelma went on. "I liked math and I think I'd like working with computers. I never mentioned anything like that to Al because he thought the only place for a woman was in the home."

Thelma had been doing a lot of observing in the present. She was amazed by how much there was to see, even in circumstances as dull and boring as she felt hers were. Now we began *organizing the facts and seeing how they fit together.*

"I see," said Thelma, "that Al's attitudes toward women are very similar to those I grew up with. I fell right in line with them and it never occurred to me that I didn't have to. I was afraid that if I didn't do just what Al wanted he'd divorce me. The way I was brought up, that seemed like the most awful failure possible. I'm beginning to see how I kept myself trapped with beliefs that I never questioned and, for the first time in a long time, I'm feeling better and more hopeful."

With growing awareness, *ideas for changes began develop-*

ing. Thelma put it together, saying, "I've been watching carefully what I think – a new experience for me. I can catch ideas that come into my head and say to myself, 'OK, what are the facts?' Do I really have anything to fear from Al? Do I have to try to keep the house perfect? Even Al doesn't expect me to be so extreme. This business of checking out the facts is one of the most important things I've learned to do! A lot of my ideas have come from old memories I never questioned."

By means of deciding what was and was not important and making many simple choices, Thelma reduced her compulsiveness about housework. She also made some decisions and plans.

"I've decided to go to the community college to work on a degree in computer science. I was a good student and I know I can do it. Al may grumble, but just going to school won't be too big a shock to his ego for a starter. After I complete a degree, I'm going to get a job. That will blow his mind since he thinks being the sole provider proves his manhood. But when he sees more money coming in, he'll change his tune."

Thelma began *applying and testing* her plans. She enrolled in classes and was delighted with her grades despite not having been in school for more than ten years. She was learning to obtain, sort and use information. She was proving to herself the power of the countless little choices she could intentionally make.

With new decisions in memory and intentional thought she was paying attention, looking, seeing, weighing, deciding, planning, applying and testing. This was effective thinking. Using capabilities she had possessed all along, but not developed, to correct crippling notions, stimulate interests, develop new activities and nurture her growing self-esteem, Thelma's anxiety, depression and boredom gave way to growing confidence and new hopes.

CHAPTER 11

*E*pisodes
Practical Samples of Life's Experiences

All living things have problems. In fact, life may be regarded as a progression of challenges. When we are able to deal with them, they may be hard but they do not persist. When, however, we find the same kinds of difficulties recurring and perpetuating themselves, life becomes an interminable problem.

As personal troubles mount, we become acutely aware of accompanying symptoms, such as fear, frustration, depression, tension and other psychological and bodily distresses. (As previously noted, these are commonly believed to be "the problem.")

Persistent personal problems (PPP's) are deeply personal matters, unlike physical illnesses that can be examined by a physician and frequently clearly identified by instruments and laboratory procedures. The longer they persist, the more areas of our lives become involved. While friends and relatives may detect environmental and behavioral difficulties, they have no access to the exclusive territory of our minds. Whatever the root causes, the exclusive territory of how we think about our problems determines our potential for understanding and dealing with them.

Some people believe their problems stem from divine retribution for past sins. Others think they erred in following their astrological charts. Many are devout Freudians (whether they know it or not) and are sure their PPP's are a consequence of early childhood traumas lodged in their unconscious minds. Sinners must seek absolution through their pastors. The astrologically negligent must solicit astrological counsel. The Freudians must get themselves on the psychoanalytic couch.

There are also practical folk who do not believe things unless they can see solid evidence for themselves. Anyone thus constituted can benefit from learning to think about personal matters in terms of observable units, *episodes* that can be recalled, observed and systematically examined.

Troubling episodes that sustain PPP's are rarely deliberately invited. Each troubling episode begins with events and interpretations that set off a chain of spontaneous habits and reactions. The sequence proceeds with little or no intentional thought or reasoned choices until each episode has run its course.

To know what took place during the course of a troubling episode, we must either know how to observe and identify what is happening *while it is in process,* or we must do systematic detective work from memory *after the episode itself has ended.* It is noteworthy that even when help is sought from a therapist, events that generated and perpetuated problems can only be known by what is recalled. Psychological personality tests cannot measure processes that unfold sequentially in time.

As noted above, a powerful aid for doing systematic detective work in the maze of memory is learning to think in terms of episodes, samples of experiences that can be recalled. Be they troubling or satisfactory, our lives are made up of such experiences, each beginning at a point in time, unfolding in time and coming to an end, either temporarily or permanently.

Records of troubling episodes are retained in memory. We can recall when and where such happenings occurred and who was involved. Mental activities that did not receive attention at the time, such as interpretations that determined what events meant to us, are retained along with other memories in chains of associations. Also retained in memory are our motivations and emotional reactions, such as our likes and dislikes and what we wanted or felt compelled to do. We can recall what actions we took and their immediate consequences. All this and much more can be intentionally recalled and clearly identified in words with intentional thought.

Recurrent troubling episodes are not only disturbing, they are repeated reenactments of the mental, emotional, behavioral processes and environmental conditions that are the problems. Because of the repetition and importance of experiences in the course of troubling episodes, many of their features are retained in memory. Persistent physical and environmental problems (occupational, financial, familial, legal) remain and remind us of their existence through sensory channels. How they were interpreted, reacted to and dealt with can only be known by recall from memory.

A major difficulty in observing our motives and interpretations realistically arises from what Freud described as "defenses." We are prone to bend descriptions of what we observe about ourselves in our favor or ignore what we do not want to see. When we are really down on ourselves, it is not unusual to bend in the opposite direction and exaggerate flaws. There is no question that anyone who genuinely wants to see and understand the nature of his or her PPP's as revealed in repetitive troubling episodes can do so, but only if it is possible to be meticulously honest.

Being meticulously honest demands accurate, impartial descriptions of what is recalled: what we saw, what we said, how we interpreted it, how we felt, what we thought, how we behaved. What we fail to see initially can be picked up in subsequent observations. We need to remember that, were it not for the continual repetition of similar troubling episodes, PPP's would not be persistent. Persistence is the problem, not a troubling episode.

Correct descriptions of personal experiences are not attempts to explain them. With PPP's, explanations are not only usually wrong and misleading, they also serve as defenses that block seeing what is truly occurring.

Habits that perpetuate personal problems and defeat us are bad habits. Anyone who genuinely wants to change self-defeating

77

bad habits of belief, perception, thought and behavior has to replace them by learning new habits. We can never replace bad habits with new, effective ones by rummaging back into childhood to try to discover how self-defeating habits were acquired. Instead we have to determine what perpetuates them in the present. To make changes, we must have relevant current information. We have the capabilities to obtain all the relevant information needed through our senses and from our memories.

Memory is like a videotape of things unfolding in time that have already occurred. It contains sensory images of sights, sounds, actions and bodily sensations. More than that, it contains representations of "inner" events – feelings, beliefs, perceptions and thoughts. Like a videotape, the tape can be played over and over. Any section can be reviewed at slow speed. Any scene can be stopped and examined closely.

As indicated previously, troubling episodes can be observed in two ways: after they are over and while they are in process.

After troubling episodes have ended and emotions have quieted some, we can start recalling from the beginning and trace events as they unfolded through to the outcome. These are *post-episode observations*. Such repeated, after-the-fact observations enable us to look in on ourselves where we have not looked before.

As we sharpen awareness of what typically causes difficulties, we learn what to look for while a troubling episode is in process. This is *on-the-spot observing*. Using our direct choice capabilities we can monitor both external and internal events. With practice we can become skillful at catching our automatic habits in the act, as they occur.

Broadly speaking, there are two kinds of troubling episodes: those that consist of mulling and brooding and those that are triggered.

1. *Mulling - brooding episodes.* While these episodes may or may not begin with something that has just happened, they are spontaneous thinking episodes accompanied by moods and emotions. Usually they just drift into automatic thought and are motivated by unresolved distresses that may have been dangling in

memory for a long time. Accompanied by fuzzy awareness and disengaged intelligence, they are likely to haunt one at any time, wrecking sleep and contributing to mishaps because of blurred attention. They vary markedly in frequency, duration and the intensity of accompanying moods and emotions. Epitomizing these episodes are such activities as brooding, ballooning importance, anticipating the worst, rehashing previous troubling experiences, mulling and augmenting uncertainties, dwelling on resentments and disappointments, feeling guilty, groping for explanations and hashing over what is right, what is wrong and what should be. They are the epitome of bad thinking!

2. *Triggered episodes.* These episodes begin with an event, or accumulation of events, occurring in the environment or body that we become aware of through sensory channels. The events are automatically interpreted and typically six phases unfold in a sequence similar to the following:

Phase 1. *Trigger.* A friend telephones to invite you to go fishing. This sets the focus of the episode.

Phase 2. *Interpretation.* You spontaneously perceive his invitation with either pleasant or disagreeable anticipation, depending on memories of fishing trips, this friend and anything else related to the focus.

Phase 3. *Reaction.* You simultaneously react with a pleasant or unpleasant feeling in accord with how his invitation is interpreted.

Phase 4. *Operation.* The first three phases happened so fast they seemed to have occurred all at once. Now you are motivated to act in accord with your interpretations.

Phase 5. *Outcome.* You have made a decision and end the conversation by expressing your intentions, either to go or not go fishing.

Phase 6. *Review.* After hanging up, you are likely to think about some aspects of your conversation. If you have decided to go, you will need to make plans. If you are not going, you will perhaps review and justify your excuse.

Triggered episodes typically follow similar patterns, though the various phases differ in their details. Events give the focus; interpretations set the emotional tone and motivation; emotional arousal energizes the emotional state. Behavior and thought follow in the middle phases leading up to the outcome and aftermath.

PHASES

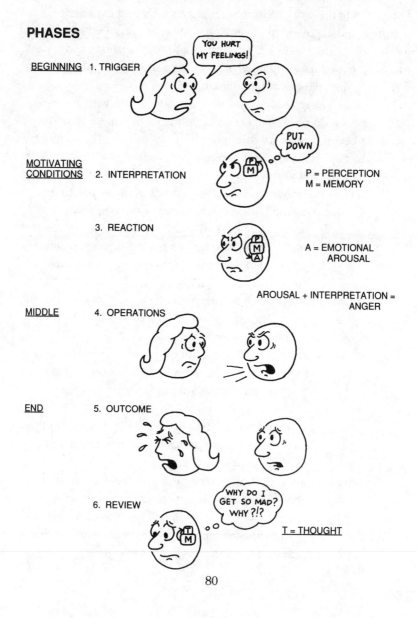

BEGINNING   1. TRIGGER

YOU HURT MY FEELINGS!

MOTIVATING CONDITIONS   2. INTERPRETATION

PUT DOWN

P = PERCEPTION
M = MEMORY

3. REACTION

A = EMOTIONAL AROUSAL

AROUSAL + INTERPRETATION = ANGER

MIDDLE   4. OPERATIONS

END   5. OUTCOME

6. REVIEW

WHY DO I GET SO MAD? WHY ?!?

T = THOUGHT

Subjective (personal) and social perceptions have their roots in information accumulated in memory through representations of actual events, interpretations of those events, subsequent experiences and interpretations of those experiences. Along this long chain of information many of the links can be distorted by misperceptions, fragmented perceptions, and discolorations of existing beliefs, leading to strange new interpretations, preoccupations and emotional reactions.

Post-episode review affords excellent practice for developing the observational skills necessary for becoming aware of how "misinformation viruses" keep us mired in a bog of problems. We can decide when and at what pace to look more closely at a recent upset. With repeated observations, we become familiar with the kinds of situations and events that repeatedly invite difficulties. These are *trouble areas*.

We receive warnings when we are entering a trouble area, whether it involves triggering situations or lapsing into brooding. Troubling feelings that go with troubling episodes are trouble signs. Like pain, they are warnings that something is wrong. Such signs provide caution: "Stop! Use your direct choices! Look at what you are doing!" As mentioned earlier, we can either look after the fact or when the episode is still in progress.

When we intentionally turn attention to looking, we can engage our intelligence. (It is disengaged as long as old detrimental automatic mental habits are in control.) Then we can ask the questions that, if pursued, will never let us down: What is the evidence for this belief, this interpretation, this explanation, this expectation? What does this behavior accomplish for me? When attention is directed to providing our intelligence with such facts, good thinking becomes possible. This is the best antidote against the tyranny of information-distorting bad habits.

CHAPTER 12

*F*ear

From the earliest periods of recorded thought, human emotions, ranging from mild experiences to extremes of ecstasy or crippling anguish, have invited wonder, puzzlement and speculation. While they are an integral part of our daily lives, when disturbing emotions occur frequently, are extremely intense and last for long periods of time, they are one of the most common signs of serious personal problems. In fact, in the old medical way of speaking, such problems were called *emotional illnesses.*

Emotional reactions are everyday occurrences. Some are good, positive feelings, as when we react with joy because of an accomplishment or feel a surge of love in the presence of a special person. Many other kinds of emotional experiences are distressful or counterproductive, the most common being fear, anger, frustration and depression. Regardless of how we experience an emotion, underlying such reactions are two complex processes operating hand in hand: one is mental, the other physiological.

Joy and fear are different because conditions are interpreted entirely differently. Joy stems from seeing an event as satisfying.

Fear stems from perceiving a situation as threatening. The physio-logical component is called *arousal*. These bodily changes are an integral part of any emotional reaction in both joy and fear, though the complete emotional states are experienced as distinctly different.

Many of us have had the experience of being home alone at night and hearing a noise that we interpreted as a sign of someone's trying to get into the house. Instantly, we become tense and alert, listen for other sounds and automatically start worrying about what might happen. Attention is diverted from whatever we are doing: bodily changes like increased tension and more rapid heartbeats occur, and if fear is strong we may break out in a cold sweat and begin trembling. Such bodily activities and feelings of fear persist as long as we believe we are in danger.

We typically describe these experiences with statements like, "That noise scared me." In reality, the noise itself is not the element feared, but rather the interpretation, the automatic perception, that the noise is a sign of possible danger. Such threatening anticipa-tions instantly evoke arousal. It is the combined <u>interpretation</u> and <u>bodily arousal</u> that we experience as the emotion.

Consider the differences suggested below. In sequence A, the person anticipates an indefinite threat from a sound, does not know how to deal with it and incubates it in thought into a feeling of terror.

Sequence A

Under the same circumstances, in sequence B, another person perceives the sound as something familiar and of no consequence. The effects are very different.

84

Because fears in their various forms are acknowledged by most psychiatrists and psychologists to be one of the most common symptoms of persistent personal problems, the following discussion will focus primarily on these highly common and important emotions.

We come into the world with strong inborn dislikes of disturbing physical sensations, such as pain, an inability to breathe, falling and immobilization. We do not fear these states if we know we can eliminate or avoid them. But if such conditions had occurred when we were unable to protect ourselves, we would likely learn to fear situations associated with them.

At a different level, beliefs and interpretations can be as alarming as the above physical traumas. Intense suffering can accompany perceptions of hurt pride, wounded egos, humiliation and lost respect. People afflicted with unfavorable self-attitudes are especially vulnerable to such "symbolic injuries." Although they are just ideas, they can be so painful that sufferers learn to fear situations in which they expect such "feelings" to recur.

Fears are learned reactions, acquired by a process called *conditioning*. *Conditioned fear* is learned when disturbing experiences are accompanied by stimuli which, when encountered again, serve as signals that the same disturbing experiences will recur.

For example, in a laboratory setting, we or animals can be trained to react with fear to any signal. This training, or *fear conditioning*, consists of arranging a signal, like the onset of a light, so that it occurs almost simultaneously with a distressful stimulus, such as an electric shock. After a few repetitions of such sequences, just the onset of the light without shock will elicit fear reactions. This reaction to the light alone proves that learning took place.

Fear reactions consist of two parts: (a) anticipation of distress, and (b) increased physiological arousal elicited by the anticipation. With animals, we can only observe the stimuli and responses, e.g., the light, shock, behavior and arousal symptoms. We cannot tell what happens inside the animal's head in the interim between the signal and the response. Human subjects, however, when asked, can tell us they anticipated getting a shock.

Mental events that occur between the signal and response (the perceptual anticipation of distress) are what old-line behaviorists left out of the picture. Interestingly, that is also what most people leave out when they describe their own fear reactions. Fears (and other emotional reactions, too) are typically attributed to external causes. Few clearly recognize that feared conditions are signals which trigger the real causes – spontaneous anticipations of distress. When we recognize this from our self-observations, we begin to understand that what needs our attention is what we anticipate.

The conditioned fear model consists of the following sequence:

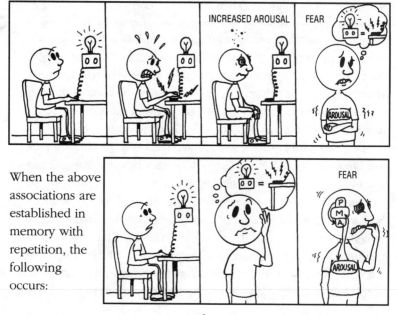

When the above associations are established in memory with repetition, the following occurs:

When a young boy who cannot swim goes out too deep in a pool, his inability to breathe and alleviate the situation is innately, severely disturbing. Because of these conditions, just one experience like this can be enough to establish an intense fear of water. If he continually avoids entering water because of fear, he cannot learn the skills necessary to protect himself in the future. Every such sequence keeps the anticipation-fear connections vivid in memory. There are numerous kinds of situations like these which we could learn to fear if innately disturbing conditions were imposed on us and we were incapable of dealing with them.

Consider, however, situations like reciting in class, going to a supermarket or restaurant, attending a union meeting, talking to a stranger or saying "no" to another's demands. These are not innately disturbing. How can these be threatening enough to evoke fear? The answer lies in intensely distressful expectations. It is surprising how many people recall suffering anguish from being required to recite in school. For them, the common danger was their anticipation of being so nervous that they would tremble, stammer, forget their lines, and others would think them stupid.

Similarly, where are the dangers in refusing others' requests? Many accede to others' demands with the justification that they do not want to hurt their feelings. Typically, the real underlying distress is an expectation that failure to comply will cause dislike and rejection.

We are predisposed to fear if we have learned to doubt our worth and capabilities. If we believe we are not worth much, we are bound to expect that others share the same opinion. If we lack confidence in our abilities to manage our emotions or thoughts, behave normally, protect our interests effectively and make favorable impressions, we are likely to feel like worms amidst a flock of crows.

When self-doubts are strong, we inadvertently convert benign situations into threats by projecting our own disturbing expectations into them – expectations that set off fear reactions, as when the light goes on in the conditioned fear model. With such expectations, we soon learn to fear the situations themselves.

Low self-confidence and low self-esteem foster fear.

How do people learn to doubt their worth and competence? One set of circumstances that particularly favors the development of self-doubting attitudes is a no-win home environment, especially if it persists throughout a child's development from infancy to adolescence.   In this setting, one parent is usually dominant and the other passive or indifferent. The dominant parent is critical, fault-finding, punitive and often perfectionistic, demanding things be done by his or her standards without providing adequate instruction or guidance. Whatever is not done "right" is punished by methods ranging from verbal derision to beatings, while special efforts go unacknowledged and unrewarded. The no-win home is a regime of <u>enforced ineffectiveness</u>. If this situation prevails throughout a child's development and there are insufficient rewarding experiences outside the home to counteract its negative impacts, the child will very likely emerge with an unintentionally learned "inferiority complex."   We saw a classic example of this in the case of Clara described in the second chapter.

As self-defeating attitudes of incompetence grow, a person is motivated by fear of failure to avoid trying to develop potential skills and abilities. Early in the child's life negative feedback loops emerge, such as impaired school performance and rejection by other children – experiences outside the home that confirm the self-doubts unintentionally acquired at home. Such budding vicious circles soon bloom into PPP's.

Primary Forms of Fear

The three most common forms of fear that cause the greatest difficulties – anxiety, phobias, and panics – are initiated and maintained by spontaneous expectations of dangers or harm that cannot be effectively managed. The sensations and other effects of intense arousal also augment the fears.

Anxiety is a prolonged fear state maintained by ill-defined troubling preoccupations or obsessions.   Anxious people are chronically overly aroused and complain of being keyed up, nervous and tense.

Anxiety-producing preoccupations, as previously described include three general features that constitute an *anxiety triad*:

(1) worry about disturbing things that might happen; (2) uncertainty about what is feared (i.e., when, where and how "it" might happen); and (3) a vague feeling of helplessness. (How could anyone feel confident inundated in such uncertainties?)

Anxious people typically say they do not know why they are anxious. In the absence of known, clearly identifiable threatening conditions, the causes remain a mystery, but the fears are real. Since we cannot experience anxiety with a blank mind, when anxiety is impairing our lives, it behooves us to discover what alarming ideas our brains are spontaneously producing.

Phobias are unrealistic fears of specific things, such as spiders, snakes, mice, other vermin or germs. Disturbing experiences in the past with feared objects sometimes, but not always, influence the focus of phobias. For example, a spider phobic may have been teased as a child with spiders by an older cousin.

Phobias range from mild to severe. Mild phobias induce avoidance of feared objects and hence they persist. Severe phobias can become crippling obsessions, especially when the feared object is not directly observable, such as a fear of germs.

Panics can be triggered by truly threatening conditions in which little or no self-protection is possible. Nevertheless, it is remarkable how, even in the face of death, victims often march before the firing squad with no visible signs of fear. What takes place in their minds must make a difference.

Panics that persist for no apparent reason are intricately related to arousal reactions and how arousal symptoms are interpreted. Since this relationship is highly important and seldom recognized by sufferers, we will consider some main features of this interaction between our minds and bodies in the following chapter.

Can Fears Be Unlearned?

Fear takes many forms. It is always to be found wherever emotional disorders exist.

If we are depressed, we are afraid: what is more threatening than being preoccupied with lost self-esteem, confidence and hope? If we are paranoid, we fear the schemes, plots or intrigues that we believe others are perpetrating against us. If we are hysterical, we fear our inability to face difficulties and control our emotions. If we are anxious, phobic or panic stricken, fears dominate us directly, i.e., fear of our own fears and their effects.

What can be done about fears? No problem can be resolved unless we know what it consists of. The boy who fears water after nearly drowning knows what threatening dangers he anticipates. If he wants to overcome that fear, he has to prove to himself <u>by his own accomplishments</u> that with good judgment and appropriate skills he can cope with the potential danger of deep water.

The same processes are the only enduring ways to overcome fears stemming from anticipated phantom dangers and harm. The starting point is discovering <u>what</u> danger, threat or harm is expected. What is really feared? "I'm afraid I'll get too nervous if I'm called on in the meeting." "I'm afraid I'll hurt their feelings." "I'm afraid I'll fail." Such answers require a closer look. What is the real personal danger or threat that would grip us if we were called on at a meeting? What personal harm would occur if we did offend someone by expressing our opinions or sticking up for ourselves? What if we tried and failed to win a game, to obtain a job, to get a date? Is it anticipated that if called on we have nothing to offer or that being nervous will make us look foolish? Are we submissive because of anticipating that others will dislike us if we express our opinions or protect our interests? Do we avoid trying because we expect that any failure will prove us worthless and cause others to regard us with contempt?

The meanings attributed to the sensations and reduced effectiveness that accompany intense arousal have an important role in fear. When we are afraid and do not know why, it is very important to distinguish <u>sensations</u> of arousal from the catchall term "feelings." Does the muscular tension, pounding heart, trembling, lightheadedness, butterflies in the stomach, or even feeling less effective really hurt? Careful observation of arousal sensations reveals that the only truly terrible features are our interpretations of the horrible things we think are happening or will happen.

Fear arises from projections into future time. What ideas do we have about ourselves that force us to attach such importance to what others *might* think or to the impressions we *may* make? When we identify the real threats we anticipate, so often we find that the claws gripping us are just ideas – projected beliefs and interpretations. Looking further, we discover that, because we did not know what we really feared (the dangers anticipated), we naturally believed there was nothing we could do about it.

Since similar anticipations, doubts of capabilities and dread of arousal sensations and reduced effectiveness recur with every troubling episode, there are limitless opportunities to observe. Repeated observations from memory of the sequences – anticipations, arousal sensations and their interpretations – in fear episodes can reveal the real problems.

Fears of any sort are always reactions to threatening anticipations. The more severe the anticipated distress and the less we believe ourselves able to contend with it, the more intense the fear.

Fear, like arousal, is an inborn benefactor. There are real dangers in this world and it behooves us to recognize them, be wary of them and protect ourselves from them. Fears of threatening phantoms automatically generated by our brains behoove us to take over from automatic pilot, activate our intelligence and connect it with the direct choice capabilities that enable us to observe the facts and put them together.

If we lost a leg, we could not grow a new one. But the wonderful news is that if we are crippled with fear we can change debilitating beliefs and correct their offshoots, distorted interpretations and anticipations. We possess the capabilities for making the intentional choices that can put into practice the "Serenity Prayer:"

> *"God grant me the courage to change the things I can*
> *change, the serenity to accept those I cannot change,*
> *and the wisdom to know the difference."*

The "restaurant phenomenon" mentioned earlier is a good example of composite fear entailing "what might happen," arousal symptoms and "what they think." It is informative to see how a young man thus afflicted went about disenfranchising such fears with a little bit of help.

When I first saw Gregory, he complained that he was so afraid of restaurants he had to refuse any invitation. This embarrassed him terribly. He did not know why he felt like this nor how to get rid of his fears.

We observed what occurred during these fearful episodes. Beginning at the beginning, he recalled *seeing* "all those people looking at me." When I questioned this, he acknowledged that he *believed* all those people had been watching him. He was in such a nervous state that he said he *knew* they were looking to see what was wrong with him. He remembered how he trembled and spilled some coffee. His arousal had soared to such a pitch that he became nauseated and had to go home. Later, he reviled himself for being such a weakling, but after several similar experiences he simply began avoiding restaurants entirely.

With repeated observation of external conditions and what they meant to him inside, he saw how these and other troubling episodes were manifestations of his own self-doubts. Looking into his past history, he recalled how he could never do anything right according to his father and how the same ideas haunted him through school.

As the picture became clearer, he firmly decided that he must work on such fears. He felt that once he overcame the fear of restaurants, it would give him the confidence to tackle other problems. Deciding that he was going to learn how to deal with this fear, he developed a plan that was both practical and simple. He would start gaining experiences in small cafes because these were less threatening. He rehearsed the scenarios many times in his imagination, thinking of such details as planning to sit near the entrance (so that he would not feel confined and could leave quickly if fears welled too high), ordering nothing but coffee or coke, deliberately but unobtrusively observing others to check out how many were really looking at him and for how long. He reminded himself constantly to check his anticipations and to re-member that he could not possibly know what others think. He also resolved to continue with this plan, accepting the fact that there would be periodic flare ups and that only persistent practice can establish new skills.

Gregory repeatedly enacted his plan, noticing that he rarely attracted more than a glance from others. As he corrected his old automatic projections, his confidence grew and he felt less fearful.

He began ordering full meals and, while enjoying them, was amazed to find that he was hardly nervous at all, and was not apprehensively looking to see if he were being watched by others. Eventually, Gregory extended his experiences to larger restaurants and continued proving to himself, by gradual steps, that he could overcome his dreads. He learned, through a process of good thinking and translating sound ideas into action, that he could obtain the facts, correct his threatening expectations and prove to himself that he could do what seemed impossible because of fear. Like a boy who learned to swim by trying, Gregory proved that he could keep himself from drowning in fear.

He chose to use his abilities to choose. He took my hints. In place of watching "all those people looking at me," he looked at his dreaded expectations. There he saw the real cause of these fears. By observing and checking the facts, he proved these dreads false. These fears were no longer an incomprehensible mystery. He was no longer helpless – at their mercy. With persistence, his efforts were doubly rewarded. As the fears reduced he gained freedom to function in feared places. Knowing where to look and what to do if the old automatic habits should spring back and trigger fear was his second, bonus reward.

CHAPTER 13

*A*rousal

Interactions Between Mind and Body

Visceral arousal involves changes in major bodily systems, such as metabolism, circulation, respiration, and hormonal and other chemical balances. These changes are induced by many specialized areas of the brain which transmit signals to organs throughout the body by branches of the autonomic nervous system. They are initiated by physical stimulation, e.g., painful or erotic, and our interpretations of conditions, whether gratifying or threatening, startling or innately disturbing. The physical effects include an elevated energy level, activated bodily protective mechanisms (e.g., coagulability of blood to help arrest bleeding), increased muscular potential for vigorous action and heightened alertness to danger. In the words of Walter Cannon who laid the foundation for modern conceptions of emotion, arousal is an "emergency reaction which prepares the organism for flight or fight."

The figure to the right suggests some important interacting relationships. Interpretations

95

by perception (P) or thought (T) are determined by information and associations in memory (M). Disturbing interpretations elevate arousal (A) which causes bodily sensations (S). Sensations from arousal are, in turn, interpreted by perception and thought and fed back into memory.

The body contains many regulatory mechanisms that maintain a "steady state." This amounts to holding blood pressure, metabolism, blood chemistry and other vital processes within a "normal" range when nothing alarming or strenuous is occurring. Should some sudden event startle us or should we perceive a situation as threatening, all these systems rapidly change from a steady state to a state that prepares the body for an emergency. When this happens, some of the changes can be sensed at once.

First we are most likely to experience:

> muscular tension,
>> heart palpitation, and
>>> increased
>>>> respiration.

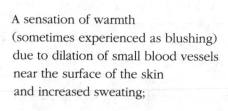

Other physiological adjustments, though not sensed directly, occur such as increased blood pressure, release of adrenaline and glycogen into the blood stream and shunting of blood from the digestive system to skeletal muscles. Some effects of these and other processes can be sensed, if not at once, a little later. Among the most prominent:

> A sensation of warmth
> (sometimes experienced as blushing)
> due to dilation of small blood vessels
> near the surface of the skin
> and increased sweating;

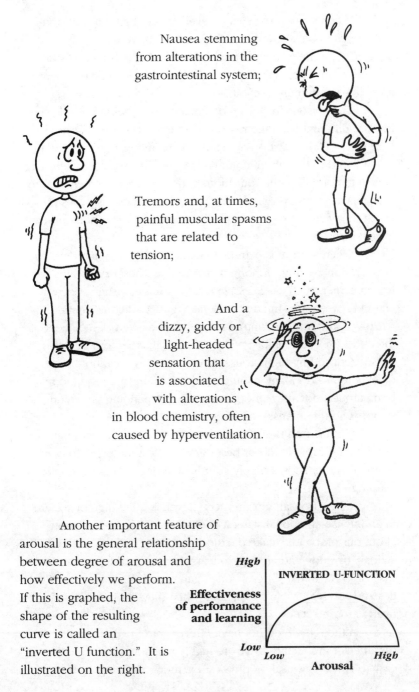

Nausea stemming from alterations in the gastrointestinal system;

Tremors and, at times, painful muscular spasms that are related to tension;

And a dizzy, giddy or light-headed sensation that is associated with alterations in blood chemistry, often caused by hyperventilation.

Another important feature of arousal is the general relationship between degree of arousal and how effectively we perform. If this is graphed, the shape of the resulting curve is called an "inverted U function." It is illustrated on the right.

INVERTED U-FUNCTION

High

Effectiveness of performance and learning

Low

Low   *High*

Arousal

97

When arousal (or energy level) is very low, our performance tends to be below par. Likewise, when we are overly aroused, as in intense emotional states, the effectiveness of both our mental and behavioral performance is also well below the level of our optimum capabilities.

The reasons for lowered effectiveness when arousal is very low are different from the reasons that it is down when arousal is very high. With low arousal, energy level, motivation and attention all tend to be suboptimum and we put relatively little effort or concentration into either our thought or our action. When we are very relaxed and arousal is low, our low effectiveness poses no threat, however, because arousal can increase to an optimum level instantaneously if the need arises.

When arousal is extremely high, many factors interfere with effective functioning. Among them are the arousal symptoms mentioned earlier, such as excessive tension, tremulousness, nausea and giddy feelings. In addition, relative to conditions, attention is narrowed and tunneled into whatever is perceived as the agent of threat (or joy). In contrast with low arousal, when our effectiveness is reduced by high arousal, the arousal level cannot be quickly reduced. Many minutes, or even hours, are required to bring arousal down to an optimum level, depending on circumstances and the intensity of arousal.

We function best when arousal is at an intermediate level. We then are capable of our best thinking, best motor performance (particularly when it is highly coordinated or complex) and best learning.

When arousal, or our energy level, is quite high or we are in an intense emotional state, it is not the time to try to reason about our problems, make decisions or plans, perform skilled actions, or study and attempt to learn. A grave misfortune in the case of PPP's is that sufferers often attempt to explain their difficulties and resolve problem situations when they are in extremely overly aroused states.

Although we do not have direct control over arousal, we can affect it indirectly. If we are highly relaxed or lethargic, it is easy to elevate arousal by physical exertion. Bringing arousal down is much more difficult and involves skills that can only be acquired with practice.

One helpful approach is relaxation, simply learning to completely let go of muscular tension throughout the entire body. However, if one is intensely preoccupied with troubles, it is almost impossible to relieve muscular tension at the same time. This is where skill at diverting attention or meditation* can be useful. People who have learned to meditate effectively (e.g., to completely concentrate on some innocuous stimulus, such as exhalation or a word) can divert attention from distressful preoccupations, making it easier to relax physically. By such indirect means, we can reduce the level of arousal somewhat, but much practice is needed to develop skill at intentional relaxation and meditation or other means of diverting attention. We cannot control intense arousal by dint of will power.

Learning to deal with panics and the accompanying intense arousal reactions requires understanding both the basic nature of fear and physiological arousal. Fear always entails anticipating something physically or mentally threatening and painful. The more overpowering such threatening conditions seem, the more intense fear is likely to be (perhaps excluding resigned acceptance of death before a firing squad). Arousal is a natural survival facilitating reaction that elevates bodily energy capacities in anticipation of threatening conditions. It is a carryover from ancient ancestors who lived when threatening conditions required flight or fight. Panic is fear blown into terror, very often because of terrifying interpretations of arousal symptoms.

Interpretations of arousal symptoms

The various aspects of arousal that we can sense are *arousal symptoms*. They are natural, normal accompaniments of the many physiological changes that are essential in preparing our bodies for emergencies. Nevertheless, they can be quite intense at times and thus tend to automatically attract attention.

These sensations from our own bodies are also interpreted

---

*See Humphreys, Christmas, *Concentration and Meditation.*

by perception and thought. When arousal symptoms occur as a consequence of strenuous exertion or some startling event like a sonic boom, we interpret them as natural and they do not concern us.

Regulatory processes of the body that maintain a "steady state" gradually bring all the physiological upsurges back down within typical limits once the stimulus conditions or disturbing interpretations cease. However, worry and preoccupation with troubling thoughts can maintain arousal at a higher than normal level for extended periods of time. Such prolonged states will be referred to as <u>smoldering arousal</u> in contrast to arousal reactions that flare up suddenly and subside as soon as troubling events and concerns over them end.

Both sudden arousal and smoldering arousal are accompanied by arousal symptoms. Both are interpreted differently by different people. Those experiencing considerable emotional distress who do not interpret arousal symptoms in ways that induce panics are spared from being terrified by their own bodily processes. Most sufferers, however, are quite aware of arousal symptoms, such as tension, nervousness and reduced effectiveness. How they interpret these states may or may not augment their problems. Fear of arousal sensations themselves always becomes a major problem for those whose interpretations flare into panic spirals.

Although the perceptions of different people have unique twists, we can readily distinguish four general ways arousal symptoms are interpreted to the detriment of the interpreter.

1. *Social embarrassment.* Self-doubting people who are overly concerned about others' opinions tend to view any visible signs of emotional arousal as indications of weakness. They dread that others will think contemptuously of them should they be seen to blush, tremble, sweat or show any signs of having "lost their cool."

When people have these apprehensions, they are motivated to avoid situations where people gather, like coffee with neighbors or lunch with fellow workers. Concerns of this sort can develop into fear of public places, such as buses, restaurants or supermarkets.

2. *Loss of control.* When arousal is very intense, as it often is with strong fear or other intense emotional reactions such as anger, reduced effectiveness results and is interpreted as impending loss of control. Frequently, this takes the form of expecting to faint or go berserk. Sufferers who neither understand what they are experiencing nor how to deal with it are ripe for panic. These spells are particularly alarming in situations that require full control, like driving a car.

Over the course of recurrent experiences, a form of fear conditioning takes place. Any of the common arousal symptoms are perceived as signals that loss of control is imminent. Such anticipations trigger a full-blown panic reaction which confirms the expectation that one is losing control. Soon, these vicious circles motivate avoiding feared situations, be they driving a car, going to work or entering the community. Coping with problems in the real world grinds to a halt when these "misinformation viruses" have usurped full control.

3. *Disasters.* Some interpret heart palpitations or pains in the chest as signs of a heart attack or impending death, despite repeated reassurances by their physicians. Many panic victims believe that their giddy, light-headed sensations mean they are about to faint, although they never have, while others, assuming their strange head sensations are forerunners of insanity, become obsessed with thoughts of going crazy.

These interpretations interact with arousal and form feedback loops. For example, anticipating heart attacks elevates arousal. This increases heart palpitations or chest pains. These sensations are then taken as proof that an attack is in process and confirm the belief that cardiac failure is imminent despite what the doctor says.

Repeated experiences of this sort – and it does not take many – also leave victims fearing the situations in which they occur. As in fear conditioning, the panic is analogous to a severe shock and the situations and arousal symptoms serve as cues that the dreaded panic is coming. "Situational" phobias and agoraphobia in particular are typically acquired in this manner.

4. *Physical ailments.* Sensations from arousal symptoms and other physical conditions, like fatigue and intestinal gas, are

101

construed by predisposed people as signs of self-diagnosed physical ailments.

Preoccupations with ailments maintain smoldering arousal which increases bodily stresses. These tensions invite headaches, stomach trouble, bowel problems, muscular and joint aches, insomnia, and numerous other complaints. Physical disorders due to other causes, such as high blood pressure, difficult menstruation, asthma, allergies and arthritis are further aggravated.

Sufferers interpret their symptoms as signs of insidious diseases, such as cancer, multiple sclerosis, ulcers, cardiac and other pathologies that are often difficult to diagnose. When physicians find nothing organically wrong with sufferers, instead of being reassured, their uncertainties increase. They say, "Why do I feel like this? It's not my imagination. Something's wrong that the doctors can't find."

People with these inclinations are commonly referred to as hypochondriacs or they are told their illnesses are "psychosomatic." They adapt to their insecurities by preoccupations with physical complaints leading to the "power of weakness" vicious circle. Physical ailments provide an excuse to avoid undesirable tasks or assignments and a means to gain sympathy. Sufferers absolve themselves of all responsibility by perceiving themselves as physical invalids through no fault of their own. Arousal symptoms can serve these purposes admirably. Many panic victims take this route.

Arousal, the exquisite ability of our bodies to provide instantaneous super-energy for contending with life-threatening emergencies, is a cornerstone of survival for individuals and species. It is a beneficence for both predator and prey. With our self-focus, language and penchant for explaining without facts, only we humans convert this life-preserving necessity into a fearful liability.

Nevertheless, there also are many panic sufferers who will not settle for invalidism. In the next chapter, we will see how, despite many hardships, Pat learned to manage both her fears and alarming interpretations of arousal symptoms.

$\mathcal{P}$anic Spirals

Fear is a kind of psychological pain. Like pain sensations, it is essential for survival, but it also can become malignant. As previously discussed, fear involves two distinct parts: psychological and physiological. The psychological, or subjective part, consists of anticipated distress and uncertainty about dealing with it. The physiological part, *arousal*, consists of internal changes that prepare the body for emergencies, for vigorous exertion and possible injury. As arousal increases, metabolism, muscle tone, blood coagulability, central nervous system alertness and other physiological conditions change.

Arousal has such an important role in fears and especially panics that we can profit from quickly reviewing some of its features. Certain of these physiological changes produce bodily sensations or *arousal symptoms* which attract attention and enter awareness. The most common include muscular tension, tremor and pain from muscular spasms; sweating and feeling hot or cold; heart actions such as palpitations, flutter and skipped beats; occasionally a sensation of choking or shortness of breath; abdominal distres, and nausea. Some people report feeling they will lose control of anal or urethral sphincters. Most people experience peculiar head sensations described as light headedness, giddiness, dizziness or faintness. A general consequence of all this is that, as arousal becomes intense, we feel and become less effective and less in control.

These are normal accompaniments of an arousal state. Their meaning to a person depends on their intensity, duration and, above all, how they are interpreted. It is not uncommon for people to interpret arousal symptoms as indications of impending disasters, like loss of control, heart attacks, death or insanity.

Freud assumed that certain threats to the ego were the basic source of anxiety which, in turn, activated repression and elicited ego defenses. The psychiatrist Joseph Wolpe assumed that neuroses were a net result of many conditioned or learned fears. Cognitive theorists, such as Albert Ellis, contend that fears are maintained by "the things people tell themselves," e.g., interpretations that threaten self-worth and that attribute threatening conditions to the environment. Whatever the assumed causes, it is generally agreed that various fears underlie the persistent personal problems that psychiatry now calls emotional disorders.

The intensity of fear ranges from mild apprehension to terror. Fear may last only a moment or persist indefinitely as waves of vacillating anxiety or panic attacks. Sudden, strong stimulation such as a loud bang will trigger arousal and fleeting fear, but, as soon as a startling event is identified and judged not dangerous, the reaction subsides. The degree of anticipated distress and uncertainty about our ability to deal with it strongly influences the intensity of fear. Fear of the dark is a good example of how anticipations and uncertainties about what cannot be seen combine and intensify fear.

Fear is a personal emotion. We differ widely in our predispositions to fear. Proneness to fear is related to many factors over the course of our lives, such as how often disturbing experiences occurred, how severe they were and how well we were able to contend with them. If we learn to cope with distressful events, we may not like them, but they are unlikely to be feared.

Low self-confidence – uncertainty about our ability to cope – increases susceptibility to fear. Anything that decreases our feeling of effectiveness is likely to lower our confidence. Although everyone's confidence fluctuates in response to many circumstances, one particularly potent influence is emotional arousal itself. Recalling the inverted "U" graph in the preceding chapter, we see that, past a certain point, the more arousal intensifies, the more effectiveness declines. People with little confidence to begin with are especially hard hit when they experience a further decline.

After intense panic experiences, people naturally hash them over, wondering what happened, why and when they will recur. Victims quickly learn to fear the settings or conditions in which such reactions happened. Sufferers develop a personal assortment of feared situations, such as open spaces, crowds, driving a car, elevators, supermarkets or heights, and they deal with them by avoidance. Before long, many sufferers become afraid of so many situations that they literally become prisoners in their own homes. Some even get to the point that they fear being alone at home. These more severe states are called *agoraphobia* by psychiatry.

Because of the prominent physiological arousal symptoms, matters are further complicated by sufferers believing that such attacks are caused by a physical disorder. This idea carries with it a hope that doctors can cure it. But when physicians report that nothing is organically wrong, bewilderment mounts to desperation.

All of these kinds of experiences had engulfed Pat in despair and fear. She had suffered uncertainties about her worth and competence a large part of her life, despite the fact that she was intelligent, attractive and a survivor. Her father was a dour individual who demanded conformity with his wishes and found fault at the slightest occasion. He was never one to give encouragement or praise to any member of the family and, no matter how hard she tried, Pat could never tell if he valued her or her efforts.

With Father's constrictive behavior and Mother's subdued nature, Pat did not remember much of her early childhood. In part, this was because there were not many rewarding things to remember. One year was much like another. But Pat did well in school and, as time went along, enjoyed some friendships despite pangs of inferiority. In her third year of high school she was allowed to date, but entered this process ill prepared. She was alarmed when she missed her period. Her worries intensified when she missed it again. She finally confided in her mother, whose main concern was to keep Father from finding out. After some agonizing soul-searching, they both agreed that under the circumstances, the only course was for Pat to have an abortion.

Although Mother and Pat used every precaution they knew, their deceptions failed. When her father discovered what had transpired, he summarily ejected Pat from "his" home. Pat was frightened, alone and angry. That anger and an innate perseverance helped her to avoid languishing in despair. She set about investigating possible ways of surviving and had no difficulty finding work as a waitress. With the help of an older woman who worked at the same restaurant, she was able to get through the first difficult months and finally settle in a place of her own.

After a time, Pat began taking classes at the community college to enhance the secretarial skills she had acquired in high school and to learn about computer operation and business procedures. Although she suffered guilt over the abortion and tended to think of herself as an outcast, it was not long before she developed a few friendships, including one with a young man named Ron.

With the many uncertainties in her life, Pat's thoughts drifted into worries about matters such as being cut off from her family, what the future had in store for her, what others thought of her and a gnawing fear of rejection. But with an ability to focus her attention on tasks in school, at work and in her daily living, plus an opportunity to enjoy some diversions with a few friends, such troubling thoughts did not become consuming preoccupations.

Pat supported herself while in training and finished in less than two years. Recommended by her instructors for a job, she was hired by a large insurance firm. While she was delighted with the prospects of an increased salary and opportunities for advancement, she was also fearful that her capabilities would fall below the standards of such a prestigious company.

Nevertheless, with encouragement from instructors and friends plus an inner determination not to give up, she accepted the challenge. She worked tirelessly and, though keyed up and over-zealous much of the time, her abilities and determination enabled her to remain afloat. She was also blessed with a friendly, supportive supervisor.

In the course of all this, being with Ron was a welcome relief that helped to fill some of the gaps in her life. He was similarly attached to her and their friendship metamorphosed through states of romance, living together and finally marriage.

After they married, Ron's disposition emerged more clearly as a mixed type. He was a construction worker, who on the outside was the picture of robust masculinity, wedded to his pickup truck and hunting, but fortunately not a swashbuckler. Inside, he was a spoiled child. His mother had always waited on Ron's every need and she accused Pat of having won Ron by seduction. As an adult, he complained about his mother's coddling, yet he expected and demanded that Pat adopt a similar pampering style.

Leery of disapproval and yearning for approbation, Pat catered to Ron, believing that what he required was the way it was supposed to be. After a day at her office, she would rush home to have dinner on time, clean the house in the evenings and be available for Ron's pleasures on weekends. As far as Ron was concerned, their relationship was harmonious, and after a couple of years their harmony produced a baby. Pat quit her job to take care of the child and Ron found himself competing for Pat's maternal attentions.

Fortunately, Ron was not a wife beater, but he had no reticence about grumbling. He sulked. He complained, found fault and was critical of nearly everything Pat did, reminiscent of her past home environment. Adding to his distress, her not working dropped their income significantly, precluding his buying an expensive hunting rifle and "mag" wheels for his pickup.

When the baby was a year old, Pat inquired about returning to work and, much to her surprise, was taken back at once. However, there had been a change. The easygoing supervisor had been replaced by a woman who, while nice, was an immutable perfectionist. She insisted that every task was urgent and that there could be no mistakes. Since Pat was similarly disposed, this external prodding augmented the pressures she generated on her own. Her arousal was maintained at an even higher level than previously and she was often tense to the point of trembling. After each exhausting day at work, she returned to homemaking and mothering chores amidst grumbles.

Pat saw herself on a one-way street to nowhere. Love for Ron was waning. As it gave way to irritation, she stopped trying to wait on him and nagged him to help with the home and baby, elevating his discontents. Tensions mounted to the point that the only relief she could envision was to leave him. While Ron was at work, she packed and moved with the baby to an apartment. After a month of working, arranging babysitting, paying for everything entirely on her own and being essentially alone, she entertained second thoughts. In addition, Ron had tracked her down and pleaded with tears in his eyes for her to return, promising to be more helpful and less critical. With this combination of incentives, she returned.

Ron was not malicious, but his spoiled-boy habits and needs could not be dispelled with good intentions and he was soon back to his old ways. After this adventure, Pat felt hopelessly trapped. Returning to her parent's home was out of the question and trying to work and manage on her own with the baby was impossible. She did not know how much longer she could stand the pressures at work and the sulky, grumbling atmosphere at home.

Then something happened. A terrible feeling came over her at work. She could not focus her eyes or coordinate her fingers on the typewriter. Her heart pounded, she gasped for breath and shook uncontrollably. Others saw something was wrong and called the manager. He had her lie down on a couch, but the reaction persisted. Her head kept telling her, "You're having a breakdown." The manager and a couple of other employees took her to the emergency room of a nearby hospital. After what seemed an interminable wait, a doctor saw her, announced that she was hyperventilating and injected a strong tranquilizer. After her acute reaction subsided, she was taken home where she went to bed and fell into a deep sleep.

Pat awoke screaming from a terrible nightmare. Ron

jumped up, startled.

"What the hell's the matter with you?" he yelled.

Pat could hardly talk. "I dreamed I was at the office. This terrible thing came over me. I was dying. I don't think I can ever go back there."

"For Christ's sake," said Ron, "there's nothing wrong with you, the doctor said so. Shut up and go back to sleep."

Interchanges of this sort recurred whenever Pat's terrors surfaced. She took leave from work, intending to get better and return, but instead her condition got worse.

She was home only a few days when it was necessary to go shopping for groceries. She got herself and her baby ready but felt like a coiled spring. Alarming thoughts loomed up: "What if that terrible feeling comes on while I'm driving. I could crash and kill myself and the baby." Halfway to the store, she felt faint and trembled so that she could hardly hold the steering wheel. Pat pulled over to the side and stopped.

"Why do I have this terrible feeling? The doctor said nothing was wrong. I must be going crazy. My head feels funny. Something is wrong. My heart is pounding. I'm not imagining it." This went on for nearly a half hour until she managed to turn around and return home without knowing quite how she did it.

That evening Ron was furious when he learned that she had not been shopping and dinner was not ready. He fumed, "You're just a coward – afraid to go shopping. I nearly got killed a couple of times at work, but I went back anyway. I can't imagine anything so stupid – afraid of a store."

A couple of days later, Pat called her office and announced that she could not return to work. Ron was furious. He inflated their indebtedness and deflated their income into a caricature of pauperism. He extolled his long-suffering forbearance with her foolish fears. Rail as he might, he could not drive her fears away. Other burdens heaped up on Ron until one almost felt sorry for him. Pat could not leave the house without him or his brother's wife, who worked and was not very accessible. If they were to have groceries, Ron had to go with her. Pat became clinging and tearful. In addition to being afraid to drive her car or go away from home alone, she would become hysterical if Ron wanted to do something on his own, such as go hunting. Normally very active, Pat was now confined to her home with no company but baby Joey and TV. These were ideal conditions for mulling over her bewildering circumstances and her brain took full advantage of the opportunities.

She dreaded the prospect of another spell. She could not avoid thinking she was going crazy. She grappled for explanations and her thoughts kept drifting over her worthlessness, helplessness, and future of perpetual suffering. Continual hashing over notions turns them into beliefs and believing awful, hopeless things causes a yearning for relief. When all avenues for relief prove to be blind, only one sure escape remains: death. Pat became deeply depressed, described by Ron as "damned foolishness."

Distress radiates from anyone deeply troubled to other members of a family. And the reactions of others to their own frustrations, whether they be hostile or solicitous, feed back and make matters worse for the original sufferer. Pat's situation was reaching crisis proportions. Her thoughts kept drifting to suicide, fueling her fears. She shared some of her despairing thoughts with her sister-in-law who urged her to seek help. Though Ron jeered at the idea, she applied at the mental health center in her area.

Although Pat had strengths, at that time her frailties predominated. Her fighting spirit, good intelligence, occupational skills and experience, ability to be friendly and freedom from drug and alcohol involvement were in her favor. But they were outweighed by the crippling effects of her fears, depressive preoccupations and all-time low self-confidence. Aside from her sister-in-law, there were no close people to reassure her. Her life had become confined, empty and unproductive. Although she had been through many difficult times, she could not have imagined anything this bad.

From the outset of our therapy sessions, Pat was remarkably communicative. There certainly were things of which she was unaware and things she did not understand, but she had not buried information with evasions. She regarded panic spells as her most devastating problem. After gathering information about her past and present life, we approached these difficulties by means that had often proven effective.

She readily understood what we discussed and was soon clearly describing important aspects of recent panic episodes. Nevertheless, between sessions, she could not bring herself to do the intentional observing and practicing we had discussed. Thus, her homework lapsed. Ron's tirades, her low self-confidence and depressive preoccupations were robbing her of incentives for trying. Ron was fed up with her moroseness and dependence. He resented her therapy. When she asked if he would attend a few times to work on their relationship, he sneered, "There's nothing wrong with me. You're the one who's sick."

The total state of affairs became increasingly intolerable, until Pat considered the unthinkable. Even suicide was beginning to look like the lesser of two evils. She had to get away. The last resort, short of death, was returning to her parent's home.

Pat contacted her father, whose ire had subsided over the many years she had been away, and he agreed to send money for her trip home. Without delay she packed and left, with Ron pacing back and forth shouting hateful things and swearing he would get a divorce at once. A friend took Joey and her to the airport where she boarded the plane and, petrified, flew home.

Her father and mother seemed concerned. Father was surprisingly conciliatory. He decided her difficulties were due to the bad marriage he had warned her against and was pleased to think that his predictions were correct. A few days of peace and quiet helped Pat calm down somewhat, but this lull in her anguished life was predestined to be short.

Pat's sister was getting married within a week after her arrival. Father, true to form, strenuously objected to the sister's intended. His injunction that she not marry him was defied and in his wrath he forbade Pat and her mother to attend the wedding. Rebellion flared in Pat from memories of Father's heavy-handed tactics. Behind the scenes she argued and cajoled with Mother until even she became defiant, and both attended the wedding. Upon their return, her father threw Pat and Joey out.

People are at best only partially predictable. Combinations of conditions and events interact with the great memory store, inter-

111

pretations and incentives, bringing about changes in attitudes and behavior that often cannot be foretold.

Something of this sort happened to Ron. In Pat's absence he felt lonely for both his little son and Pat. With no one to rant at, he had an opportunity to reflect. His sister told him repeatedly that Pat's difficulties were serious and he was making them worse. Maybe, he considered, she was right. Maybe he was wrong. Pondering such issues let a little light shine in, enough for him to recognize some of his boorishness. Pat called before boarding the plane to say she was returning.

"I love you," he said.

Pat resumed therapy. Ron was being much nicer and took her places with only an occasional mutter. He even broke through a barrier of his own and attended a couple of sessions in which he confided a deep resentment toward his mother. He believed her pampering was domineering and was resolved not to be dominated by any woman.

Now that several stresses in her immediate environment had eased, we again turned attention to her panics. These invariably occurred while driving her car. To make matters worse, she also feared public places, especially supermarkets and large shopping malls. She could clearly recall the typical pattern. She would begin feeling tense. These sensations immediately triggered an expectation that a panic attack was coming on and that she would lose control. She would feel light headed, her whole body would tremble, her heart would pound and she would be convinced that, this time, the attack would be fatal or she would go crazy. In desperation she always turned around and dashed home, where she would hash over and over how weak and helpless she was and how her life was ruined. A familiar, depressed feeling would sweep over her and her thoughts would drift into longing for death.

Before the ill-fated trip to her parents, we had discussed the rudiments of arousal, which she remembered. With continuing self-observation, she began seeing clearly how "ideas," as she put it, triggered and amplified arousal reactions. "It all makes sense," she would say, "but how can I ever get over these panics? When we first began talking, everything seemed so hopeless. I had so little

112

confidence. I was certain that I couldn't do any of the things we talked about. Now that Ron isn't dinging me so much, maybe I finally can get down to business."

We had discussions about insanity. From these she could clearly see the differences between arousal symptoms, which were very intense and felt very strange, and hallucinations, delusions and other states that characterize acute psychotic conditions. As she let these distinctions sink in, she made headway in reducing her concern about going crazy.

By systematically observing phases of panic episodes in slow motion with me, Pat began seeing from recall of her own experiences the workings of panic feedback loops: how anticipations elicit arousal, how arousal symptoms are interpreted as threats which intensify arousal and confirm expectations, and how the process escalates. From observing her own experiences, she had a practical new insight. "I see how it cycles," she said. "If I could just cool it when I first start feeling it come on, if I could prove to myself that I can cool it as soon as it begins, I'd start getting some confidence back."

Pat's idea of learning to "cool it" was a good one, but it takes work and persistence to develop the necessary skills. A few simple tactics must be learned and practiced. We discussed two that are helpful and can be acquired with practice: *meditation* and *intentional relaxation*.

Meditation, in its basic form, is learning to concentrate attention on some specific focus. Intentional concentration of attention will disrupt automatic thought. Letting go of tight muscles, intentional relaxation, helps counteract the tension component of arousal. These tactics, however, are in no way "cures." They are only helps over humps. Demonstrating to ourselves that we can make choices and focus attention on doing something such as holding one's breath, walking briskly, etc., help avert being swept away with terrifying obsessions.

The sooner any helpful tactics are applied, the better the chance one will not be swept away by spiraling terror. After Pat proved to herself that she could disrupt such spirals, she turned her attention to recalling and then reminding herself of what was happening: "What I'm feeling is just arousal," she would tell herself. "It's not going to hurt me. I've experienced it many times before. I've always survived. Feeling I'll lose control or go crazy are just ideas."

Pat was shown how to practice Zen meditation. She already knew how to intentionally relax. The problem was practicing enough to become skillful at quickly letting go. Pat practiced both tactics and soon found it was reassuring to have definite things she could intentionally do to disrupt a panic spiral. Fears would well up but she was less likely to be helplessly swept away.

We considered how she might plan her own practice sessions in which she could deliberately and repeatedly expose herself to circumstances that she had learned to fear. Applying her direct choice capabilities to observe her anticipations and interpretations as they were occurring, Pat could briefly remind herself what she had learned about them and about arousal, then she could divert attention with meditation and reduce tension with intentional relaxation.

Pat believed that a most important first step would be learning to deal with panics while driving. She agreed to plan in her imagination what she would do before going on a practice trip. She also agreed to start with short, easy trips in familiar territory and slowly extend the range. In the course of such sessions, she could pull over to the side, stop and briefly practice "cooling it," as she called it. Pat raised the concern about what to do if her panicky feelings got worse on such outings.

"What would you want to do?" I asked.

"I'd want to turn around and go home," she said, "but that would be giving up."

That, I pointed out, is not the case. Instead, it is an important part of practicing – learning to make deliberate choices that put you in control before automatic processes compel you to flee in terror. It is carrying out a conscious decision to make a *strategic retreat* in order to regroup for future efforts..

Pat practiced meditation and intentional relaxation and repeatedly proved to herself that intentionally choosing what to do helped her to counteract the feeling of lost control. She became better able to interject rational thought at critical times.

Knowing the value of what can be done and applying that knowledge in a timely manner are two different things, however, and after trying for a couple of weeks, Pat was discouraged. "I'm not getting anywhere. I still get panics when I go out to practice and it seems to be getting worse. I'm feeling afraid to practice."

To see what was happening, we observed together playbacks from her memory of practice episodes, from beginning to end. With this slowed down, post-episode observation, Pat spotted why her practices had been ineffectual. She set reasonable goals, but her approach was flawed.

Before starting she would give herself a pep talk, buoy up her courage and then hurry to her destination and back as though running through a haunted house. Once home, she felt more as though she had survived an ordeal rather than learned important skills. She had not followed her own sound advice: to practice making intentional choices and being aware of what was happening.

She developed a new plan, one that would disrupt lapsing into "mad dashes." This included stopping one or more times for a few minutes *en route* to "do my Zen," as she called it, and intention- ally relax whether or not she felt panicky feelings coming on.

Pat hated her fears and felt angry at having been grounded by intolerable panics and depressions. Now that Ron was not heaping stresses on top of her inner torments, she worked hard at developing the skills to break up head-body feedback loops and to remotivate her behavior with effective thought. She gradually exposed herself to increasingly difficult situations, always going alone to avoid becoming dependent on having to have someone with her – a need that engulfs many panic victims. She drove further from home each week and was not only beginning to do grocery shopping, small shoppings at first, but was also going into large shopping malls where she had previously experienced panics.

All these activities were deliberately planned and then thoughtfully implemented. In each setting she practiced "cooling it" whether or not she was overly aroused. On several occasions when arousal began spiraling, she followed an "escape plan" and left. At the stores and mall, escape was a retreat to her car where she could meditate and relax. If this failed to calm her sufficiently, she would return home. She carefully avoided berating herself for such retreats, reminding herself that she was practicing conscious choices. By repeatedly proving that she could arrest arousal and regain control of her thoughts, Pat's confidence continued rising.

An added incentive to her efforts to succeed occurred when a friend told her about a job opening in a real estate establishment. Pat liked the business world and the idea of working directly with people in real estate sales. She was more determined than ever that her fears had to go.

Pat's life was opening up. It was exhilarating to begin experiencing the freedom to go wherever she pleased. Before long she was working, something that at an earlier time seemed utterly impossible. Before long, she brought home a handsome commission, delighting both Ron and herself.

Pat was also changing her way of dealing with others. As her confidence grew, she gained the courage to make some changes in her attitudes and behavior. She had learned the hard way that as an adult she could and had to protect herself from unreasonable attempts to dominate, by parent, spouse or anyone else. She fully recognized that though help with things we do not understand is necessary, in the final analysis only she could protect herself from untoward conditions, both outside and inside herself.

After many ups and downs and a prolonged disruption, it took Pat about one-and-a-half years to gain freedom from the vicious circles that had ensnared her.

Persistent personal problem (PPP) sufferers who believe another can cure them will not fare so well. As we will consider next, two basic facts of life stand in the way: no one can change another's established beliefs and habits and no one can install new learning in another's head. The best intentions of devoted spouses or resolute therapists cannot permeate closed minds.

CHAPTER 15

*E*vasions and Compensations

By nature, we are motivated to pursue satisfactions and to shun distresses. Except for simple situations, however, attaining satisfactions and alleviating distresses is not always easy because interferences lurk both externally and internally.

Pleasant and painful sensations entice or prod us to act. Also, more than we realize, our interpretations and the ideas, beliefs and attitudes behind them are powerful motivators.

Ideas and beliefs may inspire us to seek lofty goals. They also can pressure us to act and think in ways that are diametrically opposed to our best interests. Beliefs that motivate us to evade facts about ourselves are especially costly.

Recurrent personal problems are clear indications that something is amiss. Whatever that "something" is needs to be identified and acknowledged before anything can be done about it. When self-confidence is low and self-doubts high, acknowledging problems and shortcomings can be especially threatening. Some people regard fear, despair, emotional upheavals and countless other symptoms of personal problems as shameful blemishes, weaknesses, or, worse, signs of mental illness that must be hidden.

These ego protecting beliefs generate serious conflicts. On the one hand, recurring fears, insecurities and other symptoms of PPP's motivate a need to alleviate such distresses. On the other hand, sufferers are driven to protect their ideas of self-worth by avoiding awareness and acknowledgement of distresses seen as disgraceful stigmas. Weaknesses must be disguised or somehow compensated for. Either strengths must be over-emphasized or responsibilities for failings disclaimed. Many PPP sufferers portray themselves as innocent victims of what cannot be helped, with physical illnesses being the handiest evasion.

Freud long ago recognized the paradox of obviously troubled people evading admission of psychological difficulties at all cost and sabotaging any attempts to help eliminate them. He discussed such strange adaptations in terms of unconscious defenses and resistance.

What happens to people trapped in these dilemmas? Unless perpetuating conditions change sufficiently to disrupt such maladaptions, strongly motivated compensations develop as habitual lifestyles.

Compensations always have personal twists, but two common varieties are diametric opposites. One is a need to appear flawless. The other is a need to prove oneself weak and incapacitated. Although each variety makes life exceedingly difficult, such strongly motivated and deeply habitual compensations are clung to with a death grip.

The irreproachable style is characterized by *over-compensations* that attempt to hide all signs of weaknesses. Flagrant denial of any shortcomings, grandiose striving for superiority and perfectionist struggles are typical. People locked into this style experience perpetual frustration because attainment of their goals is always just out of reach.

The other style is characterized by *chronic invalidism.* Sufferers believe themselves to be hapless victims of physical incapacities that cannot be helped or cured and thus always have an excuse for any personal shortcomings.

Except in the case of willful malingering, the physical symptoms involved in chronic invalidism are not consciously invented fabrications. When we are unable to deal effectively with environmental pressures and personal problems, we are said to be under "stress." Our reactions to stress are commonly referred to collectively as "tension." Continual stress keeps us in a state of "smoldering arousal" which disrupts the "steady state" most favorable for bodily processes.

People who suffer deep insecurities and attendant emotional strains are bound to be in smoldering over-arousal states. This imbalance gives rise to aches, pains and discomforts of many kinds. Typically PPP sufferers have significantly more physical complaints than average. These phycial accompaniments of psychological distresses can quite naturally be interpreted as having organic causes.

As bodily distresses persist along with psychological problems, many sufferers become convinced they are afflicted with some sort of chronic physical ailment. Although visits to physicians rarely reveal any physical pathology, many sufferers cannot be convinced and, as their preoccupations with physical distresses increase, the lifestyle of chronic invalidism slowly gains ascendancy.

In following chapters, we will look at how people attempt to operate by means of these compensated styles of invalidism and flawlessness.

CHAPTER 16

Shifting Focus
Panics to Invalidism

People afflicted with psychological problems often shift attention from complaints about psychological symptoms, such as fear and depression, to a growing obsession with physical ailments. An emotional disorder that is especially conducive to this shift in focus is recurrent panics. The accompanying frequent, intense and prolonged arousal reactions provide a prominent source of physical sensations.

The arousal sensations accompanying panics are characteristically perceived as symptoms of severe illnesses, e.g., heart attacks, unknown gastrointestinal disorders and respiratory ailments. These interpretations then can become material for prolonged preoccupations with bodily incapacities. Before long, self-perpetuated repetition establishes an indelible belief in the perceived infirmities – a belief so strong that medical reassurance cannot change it. Sufferers thus preoccupied are then ripe for developing chronic invalidism as an established lifestyle.

While not all who suffer panics lapse into this role, as we saw in the case of Pat (Chapter 14), a large proportion of those thus afflicted do. The experiences of Jane illustrate some of the personal and environmental conditions that favor succumbing to invalidism.

Jane was an only child with a doting mother who had few social outlets and a variety of ailments that often kept her bedridden. Jane's father was frequently away from home on business and had little time for his daughter when he was around. Though Jane was well nourished, plump, clever, spoiled and had almost everything she desired, much of her early childhood was spent alone with her mother. Because of this isolation, she felt quite ill at ease around other children.

Kindergarten was traumatic. Terrified of being left among strangers, Jane cried incessantly and was teased by some of the other children. The teacher attempted to discourage the mockery and to help Jane adjust, but after two weeks she decided Jane was not yet ready for school and Jane resumed her coddled, isolated mode of life.

The following year when there was no alternative and Jane had to go to school, a sterner teacher insisted that Jane's mother leave and that Jane remain in the cloak room until she stopped crying. After a few days, Jane relinquished her protest and warily joined her classmates at the back of the room. Thus, she was launched in school.

No wind, however, filled Jane's sails. Throughout grade school, her weight and ungainliness fueled the teasing and ridicule of other children. School work failed to interest her, but she did passably well. After drifting for years, a music teacher in the eighth grade sparked an interest in music. Soon her mother provided all the paraphernalia she wanted: tapes, tape player, guitar, amplifier and guitar lessons.

Listening to her tapes, singing and practicing her guitar became welcome diversions and gradually Jane learned several Country Western and Bluegrass songs. By the time she reached high school, she had slimmed down and the taunting had stopped. A few friendships developed with girls who were also interested in country music and who played other instruments. They formed an all-girl band and Jane developed an entirely different *persona*.

After much practice, the girls auditioned for some jobs and

were engaged to play at a high school dance. They spent an exciting afternoon setting up for their performance and testing their equipment. Afterward they went to one of the girl's homes for dinner. Jane felt queasy, but politely nibbled her food.

They were on the stand early, tuning and doodling for what seemed an endless time while couples and groups noisily entered the hall. Jane had played before for a few people, but never before the more than 100 she saw on the floor.

Preliminaries underway, they began their program. With each succeeding song, Jane's nervousness and nausea increased. The M.C. then announced a song in which Jane was to sing a solo. Jane stepped to the microphone, looked out at the crowd and suddenly ran off the stage clapping her hand over her mouth. As a couple of teachers rushed to help, she cried, "Please take me home. I'm sick!"

At home she was met by her alarmed mother and reservedly concerned father. Jane took one of her mother's tranquilizers and lay back on the recliner while her mother applied hot towels to her forehead. Eventually, Jane quieted down enough to tell how she had felt queasy at dinner and had continued to feel worse during the course of the evening. She detailed how she was sure she would have thrown up in front of all those people had she stayed.

"That sounds like a bad case of intestinal flu," said her mother who could never leave a condition undiagnosed. She called the family physician at home and set up an appointment for the following morning.

The doctor found no infection or physical problems. Jane's mother was disappointed. She, herself, had felt poorly for years and had been told repeatedly that nothing was wrong. It had even been suggested that she should see a psychiatrist.

Sure that Jane, like herself, had some malady that the doctors were overlooking, Jane's mother began a series of fruitless visits to numerous doctors, shopping for a diagnosis. They finally found a chiropractor who diagnosed a physical anomaly, a crooked spine. Jane felt better for a while following treatments, but her dreadful fears continued.

Jane's fellow band members had been patiently awaiting her

return, but Jane found that trying to sing in front of others made her too nervous and queasy. Her spells only got worse and, when it became impossible for her to play and sing any more, she had to drop out of the group.

She attempted to return to school but the same terrible feelings came over her when she was called on or had to recite in front of the class. On such occasions, she would rush down to the nurses' office and call her mother to come and take her home. These spells became proof to both that something was wrong. They decided that Jane should stay home for the balance of the semester while they tried to find a doctor who "knew what he was doing."

Jane became a recluse in her one "safe place." Her mother was very sympathetic and her father was tolerant. Weeks dragged into months and months into years, but no doctor was found who could cure her. A variety of medications had been prescribed, most of which were sedatives and antidepressants. Some, Jane insisted, had no effect, while others, she complained, made her feel dopey or agitated. None took away her spells. Instead, they worsened to the point that she avoided going wherever there would be a number of people – stores, public buildings, or even downtown. Oddly, she could go if her mother or a trusted friend accompanied her, as though somehow they could ward off the catastrophe she envisioned.

Several physicians had insisted that Jane's problems were psychological and that she should seek appropriate help. Both Jane and her mother resisted the idea, countering with the argument that the nausea was not imaginary.

Like many people suffering from persistent panic spells, Jane latched onto one particularly prominent arousal symptom which she quickly learned to dread. It was true that she did experience nausea when aroused, but interestingly she had never vomited. Nevertheless, the idea that she would had become a firm belief, with humiliating visions of other people watching, looking down on her and rejecting her with disdain.

With many disappointments from fruitless doctor shoppings and Jane's growing seclusion, even her mother felt something

124

should be tried. As a last resort, she made an appointment for Jane at the local mental health center.

At her first appointment, Jane's primary concern was to assure herself that the bathroom was nearby. She sat next to the door poised for a quick dash and perfunctorily answered questions about her background and problems. Jane's responses to personality inventories, her descriptions of troubling episodes and how she explained them consistently showed signs of low self-regard, tendencies to deny psychological problems and many concerns about physical symptoms.

Always poised to leave, she spent the following three sessions with me observing the phases of her troubling episodes: the circumstances, her expectations, her bodily sensations and subsequent happenings. Basic facts about arousal reactions and arousal symptoms as well as their relationships with expectations and interpretations of such reactions were discussed. Unlike many panic sufferers who show a keen interest in learning about processes that are central to their difficulties, Jane seemed indifferent.

By directing her attention to the sequence of events in the course of troubling episodes, Jane had no difficulty recalling her experiences during the different phases and what they meant to her. She recalled that, at the dance, seeing all the people had made her nervous. With a closer look she remembered that she had felt shaky and "like I couldn't play good. When I stepped up to sing, all I remember is that I was sure I was going to throw up." She recalled that the most awful part was having "a feeling that I'd die of humiliation if I threw up in front of all those people."

Jane had dim recollections of leaving the stage and being taken home. "I was real disappointed that I couldn't play with the band and it bothered me a lot for weeks, but I knew something was wrong and that I couldn't help it." She related how later "those terrible feelings" would return whenever there were lots of people around. It was clear to her that under such conditions she would get nervous and feel sure that she was going to vomit.

We turned attention to exploring some mildly stressful conditions in which Jane would be able to observe both her mental and bodily reactions. After weighing different situations to which she could expose herself, she decided that making purchases at a small grocery store would be an activity she could start practicing "to get me out of the house."

At the beginning of the next session, her mother came in and reported that Jane was too uncomfortable to come into the building. I went out to her and invited her to sit on a bench under a tree which she did. She had given no thought to our previous discussions nor had she attempted to practice any visits to the store. She was clearly unhappy and finally declared that our sessions were making her worse. She went on to say that her mother had heard of a naturopathic doctor with a reputation for helping those with whom M.D.'s and mental health professionals had failed. With that Jane announced that she was going to start seeing the naturopath and did not want any more appointments.

According to Carl Jung's observations, a large proportion of people afflicted with emotional disorders suffer mainly from the emptiness of their lives. This state of affairs certainly contributed to Jane's difficulties. She grew up in an unstimulating, bland environment sheltered by her chronically ailing mother. She was a pampered child with no skills at protecting herself from harassments by others. Jane lacked close friendships and involvements with social activities or organizations. Except for her music, she was not especially interested in developing her own knowledge or skills. In keeping with her mother's example, she was able to avoid doing many things that were unpleasant or threatening by convincing herself and her mother that she was ill.

All Jane knew about her spell at the dance was that she had a "terrible feeling for no reason." Much of her life she had been apprehensive of others' attitudes toward her and of being belittled and rejected. In the presence of strangers such apprehensions elevated arousal and, in her case, nausea was a prominent arousal symptom. It had never been so pronounced before as when she found herself having to perform before a large gathering of strangers. Had she been able to look more closely, she would have seen that in conjunction with nausea her "terrible feeling" was fear.

These experiences were puzzling to Jane and had become

more so as physicians failed to find signs of a physical disorder. Aided by her mother's predilections and diagnoses, Jane maintained a belief that some physical problem caused her disturbances and that a good doctor could cure it. The idea of a psychological cause was repugnant. To Jane it implied that something was wrong with her mind. Her mother, too, shunned such explanations because she believed that psychological problems were signs of "inherited mental illness." One can be sure that Jane disliked her feelings and the constraints they imposed, but she disliked the idea that she might be a "mental case" even more. These attitudes resulted in motivational conflicts which obstructed efforts on her part to learn to look and to become aware of what was actually involved. She wanted to get rid of her "sickness," but she wanted someone else to do it for her.

In keeping with Jung's observations, another serious obstacle in her motivational framework was the fact that her life was so empty. She had no romance, no strong aspirations, no involvements nor other incentives to stir up a determination to overcome her spells. In addition, her home environment enabled her to regress to the role of a pampered child and home became her "safe place." It was comforting to be regarded as "sick"; Jane could avoid doing whatever she did not want to do and stay clear of the stresses involved in having to compete independently. Like an invalid, she was provided for and treated compassionately. She felt no responsibility to do anything about her difficulties since she believed that she was the helpless victim of an illness. So, not only was Jane caught in panic spirals, she was also enmeshed in a vicious circle where her weaknesses enabled her to survive as an invalid, a process that Freud recognized almost a century ago and described as "secondary gains."

In chapter 14, we observed how Pat responded differently to her panic spirals. Both she and Jane suffered serious self-doubts. Pat experienced harsh, no-win treatment from her father and was thrown out to survive on her own resources. Jane was pampered by her mother, but suffered from the taunts of her peers. Pat struggled to survive and persisted until she learned to manage her panics. Jane had little experience with struggling on her own. She drifted and, when panics overwhelmed her, she retreated into her cocoon of secondary gains, avoiding information, activities and situations that frightened her.

The environments, personalities and behaviors of the two women were different. Their conceptions of their panics were different. And, as might be expected, their respective motivations to learn the skills necessary for coping with them were different.

No one knows what the vicissitudes of anyone's life may be, but whatever happens to Pat, the probability is remote that she will fall back into panic spirals. She learned what they involved and how to deal with them, something she is no more likely to forget than how to ride a bicycle. In addition, her need to be an active participant in life makes the meager existence of chronic invalidism inconceivable.

Barring radical changes in Jane's self-attitudes and environment, her potential for remaining a chronic, agoraphobic invalid is disconcertingly high. She is locked into vicious circles maintained by misinformation, evasions and environmental contingencies that confirm her crippling beliefs.

CHAPTER 17

The Power of Weakness
Hypochondriacal Vicious Circles

Serious illnesses and injuries strike fear in us all. Knowing that "there but for the grace of God go I," we are inclined to be compassionate toward those who are incapacitated. Yet, at certain points, even compassion is taxed and questions arise. Is he suffering to the extent he claims? Could he be malingering? Might this be mostly in his head? Such doubts are reinforced by the repeated findings of American Medical Association researchers that between fifty and sixty percent of those seeking help from physicians have no diagnosable physical disorder.

Sometimes infirmities provide social leverage. Many injured and ill people are pressured by agency policies and litigation into relying on such leverage in efforts to obtain restitution. Malingerers do so as a conscious strategy. In addition, large numbers without diagnosable physical disorders depend on proclaimed ailments as their primary means of coping. Once entrenched, this lifestyle is sustained by the power of weakness.

The power aspect is a type of social power. Social psychologist J. R. P. French defines the essence of social power as the extent to which a person, A, can affect another person, B, in combination with the extent to which A can resist or repel B's effects on him or her. Political, monetary and physical strength can provide powerful social influences. But social influence can also be obtained by quite different means: by weaknesses. Displays of sickness, spells, disabilities and uncontrollable upsets can induce desired behaviors in others and enable the "sufferer" to resist unwanted behaviors.

Tens of thousands suffer injuries from industrial and other causes every year with adaptations that range from chronic invalidism to valiant efforts to remain self-sufficient. Millions also suffer serious health problems, including malignancies, diabetes, disorders of cardiovascular and respiratory systems and damaged health from harmful occupational conditions. Among these people, likewise, the range of adaptations is extensive.

By no means does the loss of self-reliance and dependence on invalidism always originate with injuries and illnesses. Added to the vast number of people with genuine illnesses or injuries are untold numbers whose illnesses are psycho-social. They make up a large share of the fifty to sixty percent found by medical researchers to be without identifiable physical disorders. Nevertheless, they truly believe they are severely incapacitated. Physicians often suggest to such patients that they consult a psychiatrist, but this only evokes indignation. Nothing is more offensive to them than the implication that their sicknesses are all in their heads.

Incentives motivate us. Our most powerful incentives often stem from what we believe is most important for us. Many people are predisposed to attach inordinate importance to every distressful bodily sensation or atypical bodily event. Such belief-inspired perceptions motivate preoccupations with self-diagnosed illnesses. Interpretations of symptoms then always confirm the self-diagnoses. As this process continues, sufferers become caught in a mind-body "Catch-22."

Predispositions for this mind-body malady are acquired from many different kinds of experiences. Among these are prolonged incapacitating illnesses, influences of illness-obsessed parents, life with a parent who manipulated the household with dramatized

130

afflictions, unnecessary surgeries, and physicians' misdiagnoses. Moreover, those predisposed also learn that declarations of sickness can have powerful influences on others and absolve themselves from undesired activities and blame.

People who cope by means of ailments have been known to turn up with some strange symptoms and complaints. In the Nineteenth Century, psychiatrists were intrigued with hysteria. This neurosis took various forms, including extreme emotional states and simulated physical disabilities with dramatic overtones, such as blindness and paralysis. Freud called a collection of these reactions *conversion hysteria.*. Although those who exhibited them were often severely incapacitated, no physical basis for their impairments could be found.

Freud was intrigued with hysteria and developed many of his theories in an effort to explain such conditions. But he was mystified by how people thus afflicted could be totally uninterested in physicians' efforts to treat them. They behaved as though they had no desire to recover, a state which he called *belle indifference.*

Though few people now exhibit conversion hysteria, there are numerous symptoms that serve similar purposes. The condition psychiatry calls *hypochondriasis* entails a smorgasbord of complaints and occurs with various degrees of severity. Milder forms are common where people who are able to function productively rely excessively on exaggerated physical complaints. They develop an ample stock of excuses for gaining desired concessions. More severe cases become almost entirely unproductive and may confine themselves to bed for long periods. People in this state exhibit dramatic complaints that induce someone to meet their needs and take over their responsibilities. The most severe forms are symptoms of a psychotic disorder. In these cases, physical complaints tend to be bizarre and delusional, such as a belief that the bowels are permanently plugged up.

Whatever their source or nature, physical incapacities, real or imagined, affect millions and are a prominent part of life in many (not all) human societies. Those who rely on the hypochondriacal lifestyle find it a hard one. Over the years, the social power of their weaknesses gradually diminishes. As in the story of the boy who called wolf too often, repetition of the same complaints and tactics causes helpers, sympathizers and tolerators to lose their solicitude.

The following experiences of Myrtle provide some insight into how an average (normal) person can gradually lapse into reliance on the power of weakness. Her case was unusual, however, in that after resisting for years she finally decided to consider possibilities for relinquishing some of her ailments.

Myrtle grew up on a dairy farm where there were both good and lean years. She was the baby with an older brother and sister who paid little attention to her. She did not need them, however. Although her father worked continually, he was especially fond of his "baby girl." She liked to tag along when he did his chores, but most fun of all was riding on the tractor with him. The bantam chickens he got just for her were her pride and joy and she loved gathering their little eggs. Mother, too, was hard working when she was able, but she often complained of ailments, such as a nervous heart, bad liver, rheumatism and catarrh. At times her troubles seemed worse and she would stop whatever she was doing to lie down on the couch where she made wheezing and groaning noises. These frightened Myrtle who would do all she could to comfort her.

By the time Myrtle entered high school, her mother had become more indisposed and by afternoon she was often in bed. Her mother had ways of persuading Myrtle to finish chores she had left undone and to have supper prepared for her father when he came in from the evening milking. Myrtle did not complain, but, with her own chores and school work, there was little time left for fun. On weekends she always looked forward to riding the horse her father had gotten for her. Looking back over her earlier childhood, Myrtle reflected that it had been wonderful.

Myrtle was a rather plain-looking girl, described by her grandmother as "wholesome." She was shy, especially around boys. During her senior year in high school she became acquainted with a young man named Brian at a square dancing class. Brian lived on a neighboring farm and took pride in being a hard worker. He liked sports and was active in his family's grange, but had no interest in wasting time on idle amusements. To Myrtle, he was like her father.

Brian took Myrtle to some ball games and by graduation she was sure she was in love. Brian said he liked her a lot because she was sensible. One day he broached the topic of marriage, having decided that a good, sensible woman like Myrtle could be an asset in his future. His persistence swept Myrtle off her feet and before long they were married. After a brief honeymoon, they set about refurbishing an old farmhouse on his parents' property that was given to them as a wedding present, along with 160 acres and a small herd of cows.

After the excitement of being newly married had subsided, life settled into routines not much different from those Myrtle had been accustomed to all her life. In addition to fixing up the old house and doing both homemaking and farm chores, Myrtle went to her parents' home several times a week to help her mother, whose health seemed to be deteriorating. Brian worked harder than ever. He took a course in animal husbandry at the state university and spent his evenings studying.

Brian soon became irritable and fault-finding. He resented Myrtle's spending so much time at her mother's and frequently complained that she let her responsibilities in their own home slip. Brian's mother also shared such views with relatives, complaining that Myrtle had been neglecting her wifely duties. A sister-in-law named Julie, who had herself been hurt by Brian's mother, expressed disdain for her gossiping and befriended Myrtle.

Myrtle was delighted when she became pregnant and looked forward to the birth of her first baby. It was a difficult birth, which left her complaining of abdominal pain and a feeling of weakness. Her distress deepened when she found that her milk production was inadequate and she could not nurse the child. Brian's mother volunteered to help out for a few weeks, but this only made matters worse. She was very efficient and immaculate, and could not resist telling relatives that Myrtle's substandard housekeeping practices proved she was not good enough for Brian.

Myrtle loved her baby and had two more sons in fairly rapid succession, although her gynecologist had advised against further pregnancies. Her first birth had been difficult and it had precipitated a persistent succession of physical complaints. The third delivery was most difficult of all, requiring a Caesarean. It was more than three months after leaving the hospital before Myrtle considered herself able to be up and about. In the interim, her own mother rallied miraculously and took care of the babies and household necessities while Myrtle remained prostrate, complaining of pain and weakness.

Once she began to function again, Myrtle enjoyed her children. She was devoted to them and thrilled as each went through developmental stages. Caring for three youngsters along with homemaking responsibilities and farm chores was a grueling routine, but Myrtle bore up. She genuinely enjoyed motherhood. Even Brian admitted that she was a good mother, but continued to find fault with most other things she did. Meanwhile, his expanding activities drew him away from home more, which at least decreased the frequency of his complaints.

Aside from the children, Myrtle's life was empty. Her siblings and many of her school friends had moved away. Her father worked constantly and her mother was frequently ailing. Brian, too, always worked and did not believe in "wasting time" on recreational pursuits. Their affection had been mutually eroding for several years, and her mother-in-law's disparagements added to her feeling that she was not valued.

Myrtle was not active in church or other organizations and they had no social life to speak of. As the children, one by one, went off to school, Myrtle became increasingly lonely. Housework and farm chores had grown unbearably monotonous and boring.

While the boys were still fairly young, her father sold her old horse and got another. He also bought a pony for the boys and Myrtle envisioned them riding and entering horse shows together. Brian showed no interest and Myrtle was unable to spark enthusiasm. The pony was not well trained, but clever, and soon learned that lying down discouraged attempts to ride her. The boys quickly lost interest in equestrian activities and Myrtle's hopes of alleviating loneliness by togetherness with the boys evaporated.

Myrtle's abdominal pains returned and new ones developed in her legs and back. Fatigue and feelings of weakness increased. Her family physician prescribed tranquilizers, but when she found out what they were, she exclaimed, "He thinks I'm a psycho!" and stopped going to him.

Brian had given up expecting her to get his breakfast. After taking care of it himself, he would leave the house and remain away all day, every day. Myrtle often stayed in bed. Her menstrual periods were becoming an increasing ordeal, and her gynecologist recommended surgery for a prolapsed uterus.

Myrtle had much time to read magazines and newspapers, as well as watch television. She was attracted to the endless health and advice offerings. From these she learned that internal hemorrhaging could be symptomatic of many disorders including ulcers and cancer. Such information inspired much rumination over these topics and motivated her to examine her stools for blood. While she did not find blood, at times they appeared black and tarry, which she had read somewhere could be indicative of gall bladder or liver disease.

The fragments of medical information she was picking up invited self-diagnoses and inspired many worrisome fantasies. As her memory accumulated ideas thus fabricated, there was always an ache, pain, discoloration of urine or stool, or something else to attract her attention, activate the jumble of symptoms and fantasies in her memory and set off another round of self-diagnosing.

As the children became more independent, other ailments developed. When the children were unruly and ignored her requests, her heart raced and she felt faint. Convinced that something was really wrong, she would clutch her chest and gasp, "You're killing your mother." This would alarm her children to the point that they would cry, beg her not to die and become obedient for a while. After each episode, Myrtle would crawl into bed and call her mother or sister-in-law who would come over, comfort her and perhaps stay to prepare supper for the family.

Over the course of several years, her sister-in-law Julie became increasingly inaccessible. She had noted on several occasions that when she proposed an activity that Myrtle enjoyed, Myrtle would miraculously recover from her attacks. Her eyes would light up and she would hurry about fixing her hair, putting on her makeup and dressing. On these outings, Myrtle could be great fun.

Julie could not resist wondering if Myrtle was legitimately sick and if she were being used. As these considerations grew, her rescue missions ceased.

In addition, the children were becoming less responsive to her attacks. Left with no one but her mother to administer to her needs, a symbiotic arrangement evolved whereby Mother would martyrize herself and succor Myrtle and Myrtle would reciprocate when Mother's infirmities became acute.

Brian was entirely unsympathetic and insisted that her illnesses were all in her head. He vacillated between despair and rage. "How in God's name can I run a farm with a wife who spends half her life in bed?" he would wail. Many times Brian toyed with the idea of divorce, but he came from a long line of Mormons who could not brook a divorce in their family.

Matters slowly worsened until there came a time when he put the farm up for sale and took a job with a farm equipment dealer. Constantly calling on customers throughout the county, he was away from home even more. After the farm was sold, they moved to a small city where the boring chores were no longer there to divert Myrtle's attention from her symptoms.

The boys were now in their teens and each became more involved in sports, cars and girls. Myrtle felt increasingly useless, sick and weak.

She had been to many doctors who examined her for her complaints of everything from anemia to muscular dystrophy. No physical basis beyond the prolapsed uterus could be found. Any who recommended a psychiatrist were struck from her list. In the course of all this, she had a total hysterectomy which relieved menstrual cramps but led to complaints of incessant abdominal pain. These she attributed to adhesions. Pains in her legs and back also worsened which she attributed to rheumatism. She took hormones and had heard that, if these were not in balance, she might experience listlessness, irritability and depression – all of which she felt.

The oldest boy graduated form high school and enlisted in the Navy. The next oldest was a fine athlete who spent long hours after school and on weekends at practice and games. The youngest, now sixteen, had developed a keen interest in electric guitar and had joined a group of "rockers" who practiced as much as they could and were booking a few engagements. Brian had given up and was gone most of the time. Myrtle was forty-three and alone, left with housework, her mother, a litany of ailments and doctors.

Because of her continual complaints and the negative medical findings, the one doctor she trusted, her gynecologist, induced her to spend some time at a pain clinic where the objective was to teach patients ways to endure pain and pursue daily activities despite their disabilities. Myrtle did not see this as the cure she was looking for and told other participants that she was there only because the doctors had not been sharp enough to find out what was wrong.

A therapist at the center informed Myrtle that her problems were psychological, not physical. Her eyes flashed with rage and she shot back, "You mean to tell me this is all in my head – rheumatism in my legs and back, my hysterectomy, my adhesions, my hormone imbalances, my bad gall bladder, my heart, my weakness?" She gathered her things and stomped out of the clinic.

Myrtle returned to her gynecologist, who pointed out that her physical suffering was bound to create tensions. "Maybe telling somebody about your troubles and getting them off your chest would help you feel better." With that way of putting it, Myrtle felt less threatened and decided to make an appointment at the mental health center.

Myrtle was neatly dressed and, although obese, she looked reasonably healthy. She seemed to derive nostalgic pleasure from describing highlights of her youthful experiences on the family farm. Her tone and expressions changed as a panoramic view of her life unfolded. When Brian came into focus, her eyes moistened and her voice had a hollow, wounded sound as she cited examples of his neglect and callous indifference to her suffering. Recollections of the years with her babies brought tears and tenderness to her eyes, but a streak of bitterness welled up as she recalled how they, too, began neglecting her. She went on, "My mother is a constant worry to me, but I don't know what I'd do without her. She is the only one who understands what it's like to always be sick and suffering."

The simple question, "What are some of your sicknesses?" opened the door to a long recitation of symptoms and diagnoses. No well-known anatomical system was left out. She also cited various diseases which she believed had not been adequately explored nor convincingly eliminated. She concluded with, "I suffer constant pain in nearly all parts of my body and weakness to the point that at times I can hardly go to the bathroom."

Myrtle kept her appointment for the next week and began with the comment, "I'm perfectly willing to talk about all I've been through, but I can't see what good it's going to do." I reiterated what her gynecologist had told her, that all the pain she had experienced would cause muscular tension which only aggravated the pain and increased fatigue. I suggested that our doctor (avoiding the term psychiatrist) could prescribe a muscle relaxant that might help ease some of her muscular tension.

She was receptive to learning more about how the brain works, so we discussed basic mental processes and how we can use our direct choices to help the body feel better. First we talked about a modified form of Jacobson's method where different groups of muscles (legs; abdomen; chest; arms and shoulders; and neck, jaw and facial muscles) could be systematically tightened and then relaxed. I pointed out that these exercises give us a good "feel" for how we can tighten muscles by choice and how we also can relax them by choice.

Next we took account of how tension can be broken up by practicing intentional relaxation. "When we feel ourselves tense," I explained, "we can just let ourselves dangle, let go and keep the tensions from building up. It also feels good to relax tight muscles." Finally we talked about learning to concentrate by meditating and I showed her some studies that scientifically demonstrated how meditation can relax the mind and body. I also suggested the possibility of having a few sessions with a good hypnotist and described some of the excellent relaxing effects that can result. She refrained from that, but admitted that some of the approaches we discussed did make her feel better. She left agreeing to practice them more at home.

Important changes had been occurring in Myrtle's circumstances that favored overcoming the vicious circle of creeping invalidism. Brian's unrewarding demands and fault-finding gradually diminished and, since he was not a source of affection or reassurance, his absorption in his own activities and prolonged absences were more a relief than a loss.

Tedium and the need to escape from it had been somewhat reduced by the family's move from the farm. The power of her physical complaints had been waning for years since everyone except her mother had learned to ignore them. For years Julie had been a source of comfort and relief, but this reinforcement of Myrtle's weaknesses had also ceased. And where her dramatic episodes had enabled her to win many confrontations with her children, they wised up as they observed repeatedly that none of her dire predictions came true. Only her mother remained loyal, but at the age of seventy-eight she herself was hobbled with some genuine infirmities.

On top of all this, Myrtle was becoming increasingly bored with so much bed, television, inactivity and preoccupation with physical complaints. Many power-of-weakness victims sink into depression when their long-established *modus operandi* becomes ineffectual. They are then apt to exchange the power of physical complaints for suicide threats. Fortunately, Myrtle had not yet arrived at that stage.

Myrtle saw the psychiatrist who had agreed not to conduct a typical psychiatric interview and frighten her away. She agreed to take the "muscle relaxant." At her next appointment, Myrtle admitted to feeling better, less weak, but complained that she still had pains. She was taking the medication and practicing Jacobson relaxation, but found meditation impossible.

Myrtle's case seemed to be one of the unusual ones in which the benefits from invalidism (Freud's secondary gains) had diminished to the point that the efforts involved (discovering symptoms, complaining, etc.) became unrequited burdens. Because of possible residual effects of her hysterectomy, I referred her to an internist who was discreet in working with people preoccupied with physical complaints. The internist acknowledged some simple adhesions and modified her hormonal dosages. Her heart was sound, he reported, but he explained that it had been beating unusually at times due to tension and lack of exercise. He recommended simple exercises and daily walks, plus a modified diet. Through all of this, he shared laboratory data with her and explained how the above recommendations would reduce the problems she was experiencing.

"He's a good doctor," Myrtle decided. "He sees that I have physical problems and explains them to me. He didn't once say this was all in my head."

As Myrtle indicated she was feeling better, we talked about activities that might appeal to her and help turn her attention outside herself. "What do you like the most?" I asked. Without hesitation, she responded, "Horses and children." "What can be done with horses and children?" I asked.

After a long pause, she ventured, "4-H? It's spring. School will be out soon and the different animal and homemaking clubs will be starting." After musing about that awhile and recalling her own 4-H experiences, Myrtle seemed enthusiastic. Her countenance then darkened as she reflected, "I couldn't possibly get involved in that sort of thing all by myself."

These reflections brought to mind the fact that her sister-in-law Julie was also a horse enthusiast. "But Julie isn't friendly anymore," she mused. When I asked her to recall some of the episodes that showed Julie's unfriendliness, she said, "Julie stopped coming over like she always had before when I was sick and my heart was acting up." I asked her how she had acted at other times and Myrtle could not recall any problems. She then decided that it could do no harm to see if Julie were interested in joining her in contacting the agricultural agency that sponsored 4-H.

Julie expressed an interest and the 4-H leaders were delighted to have two women with horses and considerable experience volunteer. It took very little time to be accepted and to begin working with young equestrians. Julie could not get over the change for the better in Myrtle – her vitality and spirit. They began riding together frequently and, although she initially felt aches and pains from unaccustomed exercise, Myrtle did not deceive herself about their cause.

140

The two decided to enter their horses in the pleasure class of a forthcoming horse show which necessitated much work preparing Myrtle's mare. She genuinely enjoyed the young 4-H members and was exceedingly conscientious about teaching them horse care and horsemanship. She consulted with specialists in the agricultural service and studied materials at the library. With these activities and her new diet, it was apparent Myrtle had lost weight and seemed also to be losing interest in physical complaints.

Brian and their boys were pleasantly surprised to discover the improvement in Myrtle. Curious about the changes, they heard about her new doctors who explained things to her and were helping her get well. Her adhesions and rheumatism still bothered her, but she was "learning to live with the pain."

"I'm feeling much better," Myrtle announced one day in our session. "The hysterectomy stopped my monthly curse and as soon as that doctor got my hormones straightened out, I began feeling different. Of course," she went on, "having a good diet, losing weight and getting some exercise would improve anyone's health. I think those muscle-relaxing pills and learning how to ease my muscles helped, too. I don't feel all worn out and weak like I used to."

Since she was feeling so much better, we agreed to stop our meetings. She thanked me for helping her find the right doctors who "knew what they were doing." And with that she left and I heard no more from her.

Whether her improvements will last is unpredictable. I expect they will, at least for a while. Her old ways had lost their power and the new ways were producing physical, social and psychological satisfactions, as well as physical and psychological relief. Primary gains were replacing secondary gains. Although Myrtle did not realize it, the decline in the power of her weaknesses was her best hope for gaining real strength. Hopefully, circumstances will never reawaken the old hybernating habits.

$\mathcal{F}$lawlessness Trap

Ideas about ourselves are always intertwined with ideas about other people, society and culture. Usually they are beliefs and value judgments that are not only deeply implanted in memory but are also self-perpetuating. What we believe about our world, others and ourselves influences our interpretations – the meanings we attribute to experiences with our world in our perceptions and thoughts. These in turn reinforce our beliefs in a continual feed-back loop.

One of the first to clearly recognize relationships between ideas about ourselves and others and their powerful motivating effects was the Austrian psychologist-psychiatrist Alfred Adler. He wrote, "The individual's opinion of himself and the world, his 'apperceptive schema,' his interpretations, all as aspects of the style of life, influence every psychological process." Adler defined the various processes that maintain doubts of personal value and competence as an *inferiority complex*. He regarded low self-esteem as a motivating condition in which "the stronger the inferiority feeling, the more urgent and stronger...the need for a safeguarding guiding line..." Adler's "safeguarding guiding line" was a compensating need to prove one's superiority, a *proof complex*, in which people have the "need [to] prove they have a right to exist or [that they] have no faults."

Those afflicted with these complexes are motivated by conflicting ideas. On the one hand they have doubts of personal worth, competence, acceptability and value. On the other, there is a feeling of superiority which motivates striving for perfection. Others' opinions are of great importance, but, ironically, only criticism is the kind of opinion that captivates their attention.

These attitudes are seldom clearly articulated. Rather, they are typically experienced as vague but powerful needs to operate in a way that precludes others' faultfinding. This is not surprising, for typically sufferers were subjected throughout their developmental years to perpetual criticism with little or no praise or encouragement.

Achieving tangible goals and experiencing feelings of accomplishment are essential in establishing and maintaining self-confidence. But confidence can never be buoyed up merely by projecting appearances of flawlessness.

Most satisfactions in life stem from little pleasures. Shared affection, congenial interactions, task accomplishment, problem solving, exploration of new areas, learning new things and doing things that are fun are all tangible enjoyments. A day filled with them is a good day.

The capacity to enjoy pleasure in daily life is severely curtailed when attention and thought are dominated by a persistent need to appear flawless and a nagging dread of falling short. Consciousness ripples with fears of failing, making bad impressions and performing inadequately.

It seems logical that, where others' opinions are of the utmost importance, those hungry for approbation would be overjoyed when an accomplishment is praised. Amazingly, when compliments occur, however, a common tendency is to nullify them with interpretations that rob them of any rewarding qualities. We see this paradox as the inability to accept a compliment.

Compliments are perceived as an insincerity, offered "only to be nice or to obtain something." At heart, sufferers do not believe that they are good enough to be praised. Misgivings about themselves are constant and extensive. As in the Greek myth of King Tantalus, the satisfactions they continually seek are forever just out of reach.

Striving for flawlessness, like all vicious circles, tends to grow. Rigid behaviors adversely affect the capacity to interact effectively with both the physical-material environment and, especially, with the social environment.

Every kind of psychological problem and every compensated lifestyle differs in degree from person to person and in the same person over time. For anyone inclined toward perfectionism, a common difficulty arises from giving too much attention to details. The more pressing the need to perform flawlessly, the more details demand attention. When one is swamped in concerns over details, it becomes increasingly difficult to discriminate between what is important and what is not. Things that could be done with casual spontaneity require numerous deliberate decisions which not only consume time, but also make any job arduous.

Time becomes a problem. As this lifestyle gains a stronger hold, people with excellent skills encounter occupational difficulties. They become unable to hold jobs in their area of expertise because productivity suffers.

Trying to be certain each decision is "right" is a nightmare. When we consider how burdensome it would be to be perpetually compelled to discriminate between what detail is and is not important, it is not too difficult to understand why hard-pressed perfectionists dread responsibilities. Many highly capable people with this affliction work at menial jobs far beneath their potentials and will quit rather than accept a promotion.

As the flawlessness trap tightens, sufferers' misfortunes are compounded with anxious fears and depressive episodes. Driven by desperation, they attempt to achieve certainty by endeavoring to plan the details of job responsibilities beforehand. This last-ditch effort is doomed. Memory simply cannot contain all the minutia these ill-conceived efforts entail. Even if it could, the best of plans fall apart when conditions deviate from expectations, as they invariably do.

In the final twist, thinking becomes so dominated by an imperious need to be right that sufferers become incapable of making decisions. This leaves them floundering in procrastinations, as immobilized as the centipede who could not decide which leg to move first. At this point, depressive thoughts permeate the picture.

Compelled flawlessness tends to propagate itself. Not only does it adversely affect sufferers, but it also influences anyone under their thumb. In family settings a parent thus disposed tends to dominate. Since his or her own efforts are always scrutinized for flaws, it is not surprising that flaws are discovered in everything other family members do. This breeds no-win home situations in which nothing is good enough to merit praise and there is always something to criticize.

Parents who function this way are oblivious to the effects their regimens have on others' feelings, self-attitudes and development. It is as though maintaining appearances is a sacred mission that must be upheld by all under their jurisdiction.

These regimes are hard to counteract inside or outside the home and very effectively implant crippling self-attitudes in children. "No-win" regimes are not a "childhood trauma," they are pervasive traumas throughout all the developmental years. Many victims become adults who also compensate for their insecurities with flawlessness compulsions and set the stage for more of the same for future generations.

Demeaning, nonrewarding parents are potent forces for the worse in a child's development. Nevertheless, other combinations of conditions, both within a growing child's mind and in the environment, can interact to implant an idea that one is a born loser.

In the next chapter, we will look in on the life of a man with a background that was not a "classical no-win" situation. Nevertheless a combination of other experiences during adolescence interacted with his temperament to favor his developing a painful "inferiority complex." This inspired a determination to prove his worth with abilities beyond all reproof, but the consequences were not in keeping with what he had envisioned.

CHAPTER 19

*P*rices of Flawlessness
Perfectionistic Vicious Circles

In despair, Walter sought psychological help. His wife was no longer just hinting at divorce. His life had been going downhill for years. Though he had not envisioned himself a dockhand six years after he had completed training as a cabinet maker, this is what he was doing, filling orders and loading trucks five days a week in a loathsome warehouse job. He was exhausted from lack of sleep, and depressed.

He had drifted into obsessive planning in a desperate effort to perform flawlessly at work, so as to not lose his job. Recalling his sleepless nights and bewildering days brought a vivid awareness to Walter of how desperate and driven he had become. The futility of attempting to plan the details of the next day's work became obvious as he listened to his own descriptions of what he had been doing. He concluded that this must stop. "But," he added, "I'm so wound up and worried, I can't sleep. I lie awake all night thinking about how everything should be done at work to make certain I won't lose the job I hate."

When I saw him next, Walter related that medication the

147

psychiatrist prescribed enabled him to sleep and he was feeling a little better. This improvement in his physical state facilitated his ability to think more clearly and we looked at main features of his background.

Walter's father was a farmer who worked hard, tended to his affairs and socialized little. He expected the children to help with farm work and, although he was a rather stern taskmaster, he showed them how to do things and praised their special efforts. His mother was a typical farm wife: industrious, capable and devoted to her family. Walter was the oldest of three, with a younger brother and sister. He did his chores from an early age and, partially because of their isolated living situation, had few social outlets. With all the hearty farm meals, he also grew plump, like his father. Walter's home life was rather uneventful with farm chores taking up much of his time.

The experiences that were most damaging to his self-esteem unfolded over many years in school. During the early grades, contentious boys teased him and called him "Piggy." Walter was strong and could have trounced them, but he was also shy and not inclined to cause trouble. He felt he was different. During recess he would often go off by himself and climb a tree where he would entertain himself with fantasies. This tendency to isolate himself enabled other children to ignore him even more, confirming his feelings of being an outcast.

Physical Education was always painful. He had no skill with balls and was always last to be chosen for teams. However, he applied himself to his schoolwork and did well, receiving praise from his parents and teachers. But being "teacher's pet" gave other boys more ammunition for taunts.

Throughout high school, Walter was a loner. When he thought about his grades and the many things he could do on the farm, he felt quite superior. Those feelings, however, were dampened by an undercurrent of ill-defined uncertainties about himself and what others thought of him. After graduating from high school, he enrolled in cabinet making at a vocational school and was determined to prove his true superiority by being the best cabinet maker there was.

Since Walter was precise and conscientious, his work was excellent, although his instructor was concerned about the time he took to finish projects. It took nearly three years instead of the customary two for Walter to complete all the required projects. He finally graduated and there was no question that he had all the requisite skills. In celebration of this accomplishment, he and his girlfriend married.

Walter did not join the union because he disliked the idea of having to begin as an apprentice with a journeyman finding fault with his work. He preferred working by himself and made preparations to open his own home repair shop. Although his wife was working, their funds were limited. Nonetheless he purchased a few additional tools and placed an ad in the newspaper. A few calls later, Walter's home repair business was underway.

One of his first jobs was to install new formica countertops in the kitchen of a middle-aged lady whose stern demeanor was somewhat disquieting. She delved at once into his qualifications, the price and how long the job would take. She expressed dissatisfactions with his limited experience, but liked his price and time estimation. It was essential that her kitchen not be torn up a moment longer than was absolutely necessary. According to Walter's manual, it was a three hour job and he could conclude it by 1:00 P.M.

Walter began. He had to take the sink out of the counter well which necessitated shutting off the water. Because he thought the valves under the sink might leak, he decided to shut off the main water valve. Since the stern lady made him feel uneasy, he set about looking for the valve on his own. He looked in all the logical places without success. Finally in desperation, he inquired, unnerved that asking made him appear foolish.

With that out of the way, Walter applied himself to taking out the sink, removing the old covering and scraping off old adhesive. During the latter operation, he accidentally gouged plaster out of the wall where the splashboard went. The new formica would have covered the hole, but Walter felt it should be plastered over. By the time he had returned from getting the plaster at the hardware, it was past eleven with less than two hours left to

149

finish the job.

Walter measured and cut the formica with great care and placed it in position. It seemed to fit perfectly. The adhesive was applied and again the pieces were in place. It was now nearly one and one-half hours over his estimated completion time, but he only had to install the metal stripping and replace the sink. Walter inspected his work closely and recoiled. Where two pieces of formica joined, there was a 1/32" crack. If one piece were slid over to close the gap, the opposite edge would gap. Walter thought desperately, "Since the formica is mainly white, I could put white caulking compound in the crack and it would hardly be noticeable. But I couldn't stand to do such a sloppy job. It wouldn't be right!" After agonizing, he pulled off the short section of formica just as the woman came in.

"What are you doing?" she demanded. "Here it is almost three and you were supposed to be finished by one. I have to have water in the house and I have to get dinner."

In painful humiliation, Walter explained the problem. The woman gave him a steely look of contempt, insisted that the water be turned on and stalked out.

Walter turned on the main water valve. He then humbly drove to his supplier, got another sheet of material and returned to the job, truly shaken. There could be no more mistakes. The sticky adhesive had to be cleaned off in order to start over properly. He had solvent but no rags and did not dare ask the irate woman for any. In desperation, he took off his undershirt and used it as a swab. His tremulousness made it more difficult, but the new piece fit without a crack. The metal trim got on somehow and the sink was replaced and hooked up. After five Walter gathered up his things and slunk out the back door. He moaned, "Six hours' work and I only got paid for three, plus two extra trips and an extra sheet of formica." A thousand times worse were the misgivings and self-condemnations rampaging in his head.

Walter's wife wanted a baby, but he shrank from the idea. Occasionally, his brother and his wife came for a visit with their two children, three and five years old. These visits were very hard on Walter. Something dreadful always happened. He and his wife had an expensive stereo with an impressive panel of knobs. Walter was out in back barbecuing hamburgers during one of these visits and was unable to keep his customary eye on the children. After the barbecue was finished and everyone was ready to reenter the house, a startling scream came from the living room. Everyone dashed in to find Walter nearly hysterical. Scattered about the floor were all the knobs that the children had pulled off the stereo.

Every visit brought something of the sort: juice spilled on the carpet, a flower pot knocked off the wall, a can of oil dumped on the floor of Walter's shop. Walter could not brook children. They represented the antithesis of order and control. This attitude deeply distressed his wife.

As a sideline, Walter painted cars. Occasionally, a friend or relative would send someone to have his car painted after a body shop had done the body work. Walter had great difficulty deciding what to charge. Fearing it would not be good enough to warrant the going price, he asked a disproportionately small fee and was reputed to do a fine job at an unbelievably low price.

The painting of Fred's car illustrates some of the problems that seemed to frequently plague Walter. He promised Fred that he could have his car ready for him in one day, in time for a big date that evening. When it arrived in the morning, Walter noticed nicks that the body shop had missed which he felt compelled to fill, sand and prime. It was afternoon by the time he had finished preliminaries. By four, paint had been applied and Walter relaxed, thinking that he would meet the deadline.

Just before five, however, he came back to inspect the job and, as might be expected, became alarmed to discover all was not well. A run had developed on the right door. Instead of deciding how to best handle the situation, given the deadline that loomed, Walter became frantic. He could not allow a less-than-perfect job out of his shop. In desperation, he attempted to remove the paint on the door with solvent, but it did not wipe off cleanly. He would have to sand the door and repaint it, but this could not be done until the paint had thoroughly dried.

Fred arrived and was predictably upset. "What in the hell are you doing?" he gasped. Walter's efforts to explain fell on deaf ears and Fred roared out the driveway furious. Walter felt sick. He did not sleep that night nor the next as self-recriminations swirled in his head.

Walter's carpentry business was going no better. His wife, who worked as a secretary, was becoming increasingly discontent with carrying what she considered more than her share of the couple's expenses. The financial strain and his wife's dissatisfactions put so much stress on Walter that he finally applied for work at cabinet shops and home repair establishments. This was painful, for he perceived it as failure on his part. He accepted a job with a home improvement shop that had a large volume of business and an operating philosophy based on profits rather than quality. This, of course, ran counter to Walter's compulsions. When he noticed imperfections, as he always did, they had to be corrected.

Some of his behavior seemed strange to coworkers. For example, he put a door on a cabinet which on microscopic inspection was not perfectly flush. As he unscrewed the hinges to start over, his coworker asked in puzzlement what he was doing and why. Walter's explanation made no sense to the coworker who could see no problem. "Man, you're nuts!" he exclaimed. While Walter took off the door, filled the screw holes and remounted it, the other man had finished hanging his fourth door.

Walter was deeply hurt when he was let go. He complained to his wife about the sad state of affairs the world was in. "Nobody cares anymore about quality. My work was the best of anybody's in that shop, but did they care about that? Hell no! All anybody cares about now is gouging people and making money with sloppy work." From righteous indignation he drifted into despair and lay around the house feeling sorry for himself. Again, the financial and domestic pressures mounted and Walter was forced to reassess his situation.

After prolonged mulling, he finally announced to his wife, "I can't stand doing sloppy work. I admit doing things right takes more time, so I'll have to get some other job and do my carpentry on the side for those people who want the best and don't care about the speed."

Following this acknowledgement, Walter took a warehouse

job filling orders and loading trucks. He plodded through his days, hating every one of them and mumbling to himself about the miserable way the company operated. Despite his discontent, he was always on time and did what was required with exactitude.

Walter's self-esteem was on a downward spiral. A nightmarish vision drifted in and out of his thoughts which he identified as feelings of failure. He also had a sense of feeling empty, like being adrift in space, heading nowhere and not knowing how to find a direction. There was some relief from these horrible episodes when he got carpentry or car painting jobs that were free of bad luck and time pressures, or when he and his wife could relax enough to enjoy conjugal relations. In between, however, Walter was preoccupied, tense, depressed, irritable and generally difficult to live with.

From his self-view of depreciated worth, appearances became increasingly important. Considerable time was devoted to the lawn and shrubs. When he started digging weeds, he always saw more and more until it was a struggle to make him quit. Although his lawn looked almost like a carpet, he felt no satisfaction from his efforts. The same was true with the car which he kept spotless and polished. He was haunted with strong feelings that anything of his had to be in perfect shape or "they" would regard him with an unbearable contempt.

Walter became increasingly concerned with things being right inside his home as well. Both he and his wife worked, but Walter subscribed to antiquated ideas about men's vs. women's roles. Anything amiss inside his home was, therefore, his wife's responsibility. He would upbraid her for leaving lights on unnecessarily or for failing to keep the refrigerator clean. Disorder, dust, spider webs, smudges, dirty windows, unwashed dishes and clothes not properly hung all triggered disturbing perceptions. His wife repeatedly told him to take care of things himself if they bothered him so much, which set off squabbles, followed by angry thoughts and sulking on Walter's part.

As time dragged on, conditions worsened. Walter was calling into work pleading sick and his employers began complaining about his excessive absenteeism. His wife was becoming more and more resentful of his fault-finding, fussiness and nagging, and

153

on a couple of occasions she left him with threats of divorce. His sideline enterprises were bringing in little income. Decision making was becoming increasingly difficult. His meticulousness increased to the degree that every undertaking became an ordeal. As a consequence, he would put off starting jobs until he was overwhelmed with the mountain of things he felt he should do. Many things that seemed vitally important were left undone. Self-recriminations swarmed in his head, stinging him with guilt and swelling his self-doubts.

Now that it was in jeopardy, his warehouse job was being drawn into his expanding world of uncertainties. He began detailed planning of moment-by-moment activity in an effort to preclude any criticism of his work. He lay awake at night and traced each step for completing the next-day's assignments. Although the job was quite routine, unanticipated delays could alter the day's schedule and the employees were expected to adapt. Walter would struggle out of bed exhausted from his nightlong plotting. He would arrive blurry-eyed at work and go to his first post, only to discover that materials he counted on had not been ordered or delivered. Conditions invariably did not correspond with his elaborate plans, which would throw Walter into a near panic.

Life was disintegrating. He was put on probation at work. On one hand, he looked forward to terminating a job he despised, but on the other he dreaded the prospect of being unemployed and dependent on his wife's income except for a few side jobs. His wife's dissatisfactions were rapidly mounting as was the frequency of their quarrels. Walter had no enjoyments and he became progressively more preoccupied with themes of failure and hopelessness. He felt miserable, did not understand why and was totally at a loss regarding how he could begin looking for the causes.

As he groped blindly for answers that never came, his wife delivered an ultimatum. "Either you get some help with the mess your life has become or I'm leaving permanently." This demand came almost as a relief to Walter. She offered to make an appointment for him at the mental health center, telling him that all he needed to do was go. He did.

After we had discussed the highlights of his background and

looked at samples of troubling episodes, we concentrated on processes that were perpetuating his problems. We began looking more closely at interpretations, arousal and motivating conditions that constituted what he called his feelings. Particular attention was paid to the "compelled feelings" that seemed to force him so often into self-defeating behavior.

"These feelings come over me, " he said, "like a fear that I'm being watched. If everything isn't right, I'll be a failure and I'll be wiped out."

"Wiped out?" I asked. Walter shut his eyes and after a moment said, "Piggy Walter! I have so many memories of always being hurt and made to feel like I was nothing, an outcast. I can't stand everybody thinking I'm nothing. I have to prove to everybody that I'm at least as good as they are."

Between sessions, Walter was learning to distinguish between how he interpreted situations and what was actually involved. He was training himself to stop when compelled feelings welled up and observe how he was interpreting the situation. With the lawn, for example, he saw how its appearance assumed a significance beyond reason. "It has always seemed like it would be a terrible disgrace," he said, " if my lawn wasn't perfect. I have this strange idea that people will think I'm a hick. Now that I'm starting to look at that notion, I can tell myself two things. I can never know what 'they' think and, if 'they' do think bad thoughts about me, their thoughts cannot possibly harm me. When I remind myself of these things, I don't feel quite so desperate."

Walter was also discovering that a feeling of urgency often made matters worse.

"When I have a bunch of things to do, I get this idea that I've got to get everything done immediately. That puts me into a real bind, because I also have to make sure everything's right. I can't have it both ways, but I feel like I should."

"I'm beginning to see what happens. I can't possibly do everything I feel I should. I get so uptight and worry so much about what I should do that I can't use my good sense. I don't know why I never saw this before. Finally I'm learning to stop and look to see what's happening."

155

At times powerful old habits overwhelmed Walter to the point he would despair of ever overcoming them. Nevertheless, his determination was strong enough that he could make himself struggle free of his desperation and take up where he left off. With every such comeback, he saw more, understood better and gained more confidence in achieving the changes he knew must be made.

In our sessions we often turned attention to re-examining typical troubling episodes. We considered, for example, possible effects of interpreting a situation differently. Starting at the beginning, Walter would reenact the episode and imagine how it might have turned out had his "feelings" been different. He often found that a different interpretation would have transformed a tempest into a breeze. The episode with the stereo knobs illustrates this. "I know that knobs can come off without hurting a set," he said. "If I'd reminded myself of that and just put them back on, I could have proven to myself that no harm was done and I wouldn't have blown my stack, making my brother and his wife so uncomfortable. No wonder they don't come over very often."

"I jump to conclusions too often that if things aren't right they are ruined. That's why kids make me so nervous. They always make some disorder that seems like a disaster to me. If I'm going to stay married and have a normal life, I'm really going to have to change my way of seeing things."

Walter weighed the effects of different interpretations in other troubling episodes.

Among other "disasters," we reworked the episode involving the paint job on Fred's car. "All I had to do," he reflected, "was to tell Fred there was a little run. He could have brought the car back in a day or two and I could have sanded it and repainted the door with no fuss. If I had only stopped, seen how I was blowing everything out of proportion, and then used some common sense, I could have turned so many messes into okay experiences."

Walter was learning to respond to his compelled, urgent, overwhelmed feelings as trouble signs – signals to stop, look, and see the interpretations that created them. He was discovering that when he chose to recall how he was interpreting a situation and saw with his good sense how unrealistic it was, he was able to do some good thinking, size up what was involved and then intentionally apply his skills effectively.

New feelings were occurring – feelings of success and accomplishment. It was exciting. He, himself, was doing things effectively by means of his own deliberate choices. He could take credit for what was accomplished, while that had never been the case when he was driven by blind automatic compulsions. These new feelings inspired him to practice his new "head skills," as he called them, in real earnest. Positive feedback loops were beginning to replace the negative ones.

Walter was hired to put wood paneling on the walls and formica on the counters in a dentist's reception area. It was a job that many people would see and he believed that it might lead to other jobs in professional offices. He was strongly motivated to do it well. In addition, there was a time limit: it had to be done on a Sunday when the office was closed.

Walter prepared well. He did his measurements and got his materials together during the week. He thought carefully about his self-defeating tendencies and how he could protect himself from them. He reminded himself many times to stop as soon as he detected any of the old compulsive feelings and to recall and identify the expectations they involved. He reminded himself to carefully reevaluate the circumstances in practical terms, such as effort, time and importance, and to then guide his actions with deliberate choices.

On Sunday, Walter went to the office and began work. Before long a feeling of urgency swept over him. It seemed he could not possibly finish the job on time. At this point, he checked himself. He stopped and did an assessment. He asked himself about the consequences should he not finish on time. "I can definitely get the counters done," he concluded. "As for the wall paneling, if one or two of the walls are not finished, it won't look any worse than it does now. If necessary, I can come back for an evening or two and finish up." As simple as that might seem, this explicit reminder of practical, tangible choices was a new experience for Walter. It was reassuring and it took precedence over the murky fears of being judged incompetent. He intentionally relaxed and continued working.

Everything proceeded well until he neared the end of re-placing the old countertops. When he put the last strip on the back edge of the counter, he was alarmed to find it had been cut about an eighth of an inch too short. Old panics flashed. "I don't have enough material left to cut another strip. It's Sunday and my supplier isn't open. Everything is wrecked!"

The surge of fear and tension was his cue to stop and look. Plugging in his rational mind, he reasoned that he could easily fill the gap with a white filler and it would be unnoticeable. This done he turned his attention to the paneling and continued his work without problems. Nonetheless, he did experience periodic uneasy feelings that seemed to catch him "for no apparent reason." Each time, he would stop and recall the thoughts behind them. He would then recognize them as old apprehensions and move on, amused with a new awareness of the absurdity of his picayune concerns.

Walter worked until nine o'clock that evening. The back wall remained unfinished. Though tired, his impulse was to get a large container of coffee and make himself finish the job that night. This impulse was a signal to stop and evaluate the situation – to in-tentionally pay attention and turn on his awareness. He reminded himself that he could complete the job another evening and that the urgency was unrealistic. When he left for home shortly thereafter, though very tired, he was enjoying his completely new feeling, one of accomplishment and control.

A few days later when he went to the office to pick up his check, the dentist himself gave it to him, saying, "You did a beauti-ful job. We are delighted with your work." Walter caught himself thinking as he left, "He just wants to be nice. Wait until he sees the cracks between the panels and that patch on the back of the counter." As soon as he became conscious of these notions, he engaged his intelligence and replaced them with common-sense reality. Then his new feeling of accomplishment stirred – he could really do something about unwanted "feelings."

Walter was making progress. To be sure, more practice and experience were necessary to establish his new skills. He needed many more outcomes that he could see as achievements to bolster his confidence, but most important, he was no longer floundering. He was learning to think effectively, to obtain information, to apply and test decisions and plans. He was gaining a practical understanding of his difficulties. The vicious circles that had been perpetuating his distress were beginning to yield as he exercised his ability to stop, look, see and make intentional choices.

Looking back, Walter recounted an image that represented his problems. It seemed he had been living on a stage, perpetually endeavoring to elicit approval from a phantom audience that could not care less about his punctilious trivia. No wonder he felt he could never win!

A few months before Walter had sought help, he had been near disaster. Environmental conditions, mental processes, emotional-mood states, behavior, and his ability to produce effective outcomes had all deteriorated. Had he not been able to stop the obsessive planning with the aid of medication, guidance and determination, he would have lost his job and quite likely his wife. Actual failure of that magnitude would have added sufficient impetus to his demeaning preoccupations to have plunged him into a black hole of depressive hopelessness.

Walter's courage grew and he began applying for jobs in the trade for which he had been trained. It was not always easy. Feelings of failure would crop up when applications were turned down, but he knew their source and how to keep automatic stewing from getting out of control. Managing malignant thought enabled him to persist until he ultimately was hired as a cabinet maker in a large naval yard. In this setting, he would not be hampered by urgent pressures to produce for profits. Walter had at last found a place where he could practice his skills and work on consolidating his new approach to living.

His work was good and others could recognize this. When he received a compliment, he made it a point to accept it graciously and remind himself that it was sincere. Gradually, it became more natural and less forced.

Vicious circles had dominated Walter's life. With help he had learned how to effectively use his own capabilities to extricate himself from old ideas and habits that were constricting him like a boa. With less attention captivated by distresses, more was available to enjoy the many skills he already had and to explore new territories. He also became familiar with the simple truth that other people were far more interested in their own affairs than in trying to find fault with his.

CHAPTER 20

*I*n a Nutshell

Although emotional problems of different people may be given the same diagnosis, the uniqueness of each person is striking. Every individual has his or her own particular combination of circumstances, uncertainties and habits to contend with. Like snow crystals, we are all different, but yet alike in major ways. We have our joys and sorrows. We all must contend with tangible realities – material issues, health, and always relations with others. We also must contend with our uniquely human mental world – a strange world of beliefs, meanings, explanations – a world that operates with old habits while continually accumulating new information.

The beliefs and interpretations in our mental world need careful monitoring. Their influences can be dangerous. They can burden life with fear, despair, turmoil and self-defeating behavior that is all cost without benefit. When we do not understand what causes such disturbances nor what can be done about them, uncertainties and helplessness add momentum to vicious circles that cycle spontaneously, unseen.

Different influences in our environments contribute to acquiring detrimental beliefs and habits. As we considered earlier, certain features of our big brains also leave us uniquely vulnerable to taking in and retaining information that is harmful to our mental health. The following three are especially significant in this regard:

1. Our huge memories automatically and indiscriminately store vast amounts of information. Unfortunately, damaging ideas are as readily retained as is enlightening and useful knowledge.

2. Our brains have a unique ability to represent information symbolically and to reason with symbolic information. The most extensively used symbols are words – innocuous sounds or signs. But words have a power to hurt us, even worse than sticks and stones. Our symbolic capabilities leave us wide open to verbal abuse and degradation as well to false and damaging ideas. Our verbal abilities also make it easy for each of us to deceive ourselves with exaggerations, falsifications, explanations and excuses.

3. Our brains interpret sensory input by means of perceptions and thoughts. Most of these interpretations are based on information retained in memory. These mental activities, like actions, become habitual and automatic with practice and repetition. When their automatic interpretations are based on distorted misinformation from memory, they act as self-fulfilling prophesies that confirm the misinformation on which they are based.

In earlier descriptions of sufferers' experiences we saw many examples of beliefs, interpretations and expectations that were unrealistic and disturbing. The misleading ideas behind these were firmly entrenched in memory, accepted without question, reiterated in spontaneous perceptions and thoughts, and manifested in emotions and disadvantageous actions.

The causes of emotional problems have long puzzled not only sufferers, but professionals as well. Many theories have been devised in attempts to explain them. One highly influential theory assumes that emotional problems develop from traumas in early childhood. It is contended, however, that sufferers cannot be aware of these "original causes" without specialized assistance because they had been repressed into "the unconscious."

These assumptions have contributed to a belief, which

persists to this day in various circles, that childhood experiences must be explored in detail in order to identify the original sources of problems. If information from the past continues to influence our functioning as adults, it must be retained in memory, whether or not we can recall it. Thus therapists of various persuasions often devote considerable time to ferreting out memories of childhood misfortunes.

This belief is unfortunate. There is no question that childhood is an especially vulnerable period and that much damage can occur then. Certain childhood experiences can cause specific, persistent problems, as in the case of the boy whose stepmother repeatedly attempted to drown him. Most detrimental early experiences, however, are not that specific in their effects. They warp self and social attitudes and instill fixated biases, beliefs and habits that emerge later in unpredictable ways. In addition, childhood memories contain many inaccuracies. At best, they can only suggest some of the experiences from which disadvantageous tendencies *originated*. Even accurate understanding of how our self-defeating tendencies originated can never by itself change them!

The real problem with our uniquely human difficulties is their persistence in the present, regardless of how they originated. Dealing effectively with PPP's requires understanding what causes disturbing episodes to continually recur. Many different conditions can be responsible. They always entail some kinds of troubles in the tangible world, usually involving other people, and misinformation stored and generated in the mental world. Neither of these major sources of difficulties is "unconscious."

The combinations of causes remain unrecognized because sufferers do not know how to observe their own experiences. Few people appreciate the power of how we interpret events. Few know that our primary interpretive processes, perception and thought, record in memory and can be recalled and hence identified. Likewise, almost no one looks for combinations of events involving environment, mind, body and behavior that influence each other and feed back to reinforce the beliefs behind the whole sequence. The attention of most sufferers, when trying to understand their problems, is captivated by rummaging in childhood memories.

163

Many people suffering from emotional problems develop what Freud called "defenses." Such defenses keep people from seeking information that could help them understand and do something constructive about their difficulties.

We looked at a few of the compensated lifestyles that evolved in people who defended themselves at all cost from acknowledging any "mental" problems. A large proportion of sufferers put more effort into disclaiming their problems than in taking constructive efforts to alleviate them.

Nevertheless, there are many people who truly want to understand and overcome the causes of their PPP's. A major drawback is that few have sound information about what is involved in these uniquely human problems and where and how to look in order to see what is happening. Many conditions contribute to this state of affairs, such as the following:

1. The mental health field is awash with conflicting theories and therapies from professional disciplines and pop celebrities alike.

2. Effective self-observation is a subject never taught in school. We each are the only ones who can observe our subjective experiences, our interpretations, memories and emotions. Moreover, we were not instructed about our direct choice capabilities which make such observations possible.

3. The concept of vicious circles is an old one. The mental health literature, however, has given little recognition to the problem-perpetuating power of vicious circles. Certainly few sufferers think to look for such cycling activities in themselves. In addition, observing such series of events is complicated by the fact that several different modalities are involved. For example: **belief** A causes **perception** B which causes **emotinal reaction** C which motivates **behavior** D which causes **outcome** E which feeds back and confirms **belief** A, thus:

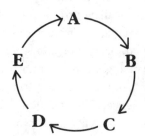

This illustrates the kinds of sequential events that make up troubling episodes which, as they keep recurring, are PPP's.

4. One of the most important obstacles to seeing what happens in the course of troubling episodes is a failure to recognize that all sensory input – everything we see, hear, and so on – is sponstaneously interpreted. When we do not understand why we reacted to a situation as we did, it is usually because we did not determine what it meant to us, how our perception and thought interpreted it.

5. Another seriously neglected feature of our interpretive processes is their automaticity. Perception is always instantaneous and automatic. A major part of our thinking also occurs automatically without our choosing to think. Thus, if a troubling feeling creeps in, a feeling of fear or despair, and we do not know how we interpreted an event or what we are thinking, then the feeling is bewildering. Such bewildering feelings inspire groping for explanation. When we know the interpretation that set off the feeling, no further explanation is needed.

6. A third matter of great importance that is related to interpretations and automatic mental processes concerns our ability to observe these elusive actiivities. It is simplicity itself. Both our perceptions and thoughts record in memory. To see how we are interpreting a situation, we merely need recall how we perceived it and/or how we thought about it.

7. As with not seeing the forest for the trees, sufferes cannot see the problems for the feelings. Beliefs, interpretations, emotions, desires, sensations all lose their unique significance by being lumped together as "feelings." Sufferers frequently complain that they cannot understand their terrible feelings. How can they? We cannot understand a hodgepodge. "Feelings" cannot be understood without looking at the parts they are made of.

8. The U. S. is awash in expert advice. Two widely dispensed exhortations are: "Get your feelings out!" and "Don't hold your feelings in!" This instruction emanates from the theory that emotional problems are the consequences of repressed traumas and that recovery requires making such traumas conscious. Since "feelings" is a word of multiple meanings, sufferers are confused. What

is it they should get out: anger, opinions, sorrow, fear, sensations, passions? How does one "get them out" – rant, whimper, emit "primal screams"? Indiscriminately? Looking beyond the theory of buried traumas, we find PPP's festering from preoccupations with traumas. Is learning to eliminate such preoccupations holding feelings in?

Emotional feelings, nevertheless, can be quite useful. Since they tend to attract attention, such feelings are excellent alarm signals that a troubling episode is underway. As we saw in Chapter 11, each troubling episode unfolds in sequences that involve environmental situations, interpretations, emotional reactions, behaviors and their consequences. Recurrent troubling episodes provide excellent examples of vicious circles in operation. Since similar episodes keep recurring over and over (hence PPP's) there are unlimited opportunities to observe features of their sequences.

Moreoever, we find that the different components of the sequences are retained in memory. Therefore, if we did not look in on an episode in process, we can do so later by recalling the chain of events. As we become familiar with these disturbing experiences that make up our problems, we can learn to catch ourselves in the act. Troubled feelings are the signals that can alert us. When we pay attention to what is happening, we can take over from old automactic habits with deliberate choices guided by our common sense.

As we start looking instead of wondering, we learn to replace floundering with "whys" by observing what takes place in the physical world that includes our environment, bodies and behavior and in our subjective world of interpretations, thoughts and memories. By our own observations we learn that we can see and understand. PPP sufferers who do so are amazed to discover that they are not crazy at all, that they are just people just like the Joneses, but with more severe frustrations in some areas.

We use our direct choices to gain understanding and our understanding to guide new choices. As we continue thus, observing, getting facts and applying understanding, we gain confidence that we can learn to make effective choices with regard to not only PPP's, but other facets of our lives as well.

The cells of our bodies, the brains in our heads, and we as whole persons operate with information. Of all creatures, we are the most supremely endowed to obtain and utilize information. Every person who is functioning effectively in any area of endeavor does so by obtaining, understanding and applying information. We are born with the potential capabilities for operating thus. Our survival depends on it. They are the capabilities we are free to use however we choose – the only capabiliteis that we can directly control: attention, recall, thought and action. These made possible the discoveries, inventions and creations that were passed on to us over the millennia. These are the capabilities that made it possible for us to become acquainted with our environment – to learn what's what, how things go together and what we can and cannot do. They also are the capabilities that can enable us to become ac- quainted with ourselves, our mental worlds, our unseen vicious circles and what we can do to tame them.

References

Anderson, John R., and Bower, Gordon H. *Human Associative Memory.* New York: Wiley, 1973.

Angyal, Andras. *Neurosis and Treatment.* New York: Wiley, 1965.

Ansbacher, H., and Ansbacher, R. *The Individual Psychology of Alfred Adler.* New York: Basic Books, 1956.

Arnold, Magda. *Emotion and Personality.* New York: Columbia U. Press, 1960, 2 Vols.

Arnold, Magda. "Brain Function in Emotions: A Phenomenological Analysis," in Black, Perry (Ed.), *Physiological Correlates of Emotion.* New York: Academic Press, 1970.

Ausubel, D. P. "Cognitive Structure and the Facilitation of Meaningful Verbal Learning," in Anderson, R. C., and Ausubel, D. P., *Readings in the Psychology of Cognition.* New York: Rinehart and Winston, 1966.

Bandura, A. "Self-Efficacy Mechanism in Human Agency," *American Psychologist,* 37 (1982), 122-147.

Bartley, S. Howard. *Principles of Perception.* New York: Harper & Row, 1969. 2nd Ed.

Beck, Aaron. *Cognitive Therapy and the Emotional Disorders.* New York: International U. Press, 1976.

Bronowski, J. "The Logic of the Mind," *American Scientist,* 54, (1966), 1-14.

Bruner, J. S., Goodnow, J. J., and Austin, G. A. *A Study of Thinking.* New York: Wiley, 1956.

Bruner, J. S. "On Perceptual Readiness," *Psychological Review,* 64 (1957), 123-152.

Buck, Ross W. *Human Motivation and Emotion.* New York: Wiley, 1976.

Cofer, C. N., and Appley, M. H. *Motivation: Theory and Research.* New York: Wiley, 1964.

Dewey, John. *How We Think.* Boston: D. C. Heath, 1933.

Dubos, Rene. *Mirage of Health.* Garden City, New York: Doubleday, 1961.

Duffy, Elizabeth. *Activation and Behavior.* New York: Wiley, 1964.

Ellis, Albert. *Reason and Emotion in Psychotherapy.* New York: Lyle Stuart, 1962.

Ellenberger, Henri F. *The Discovery of the Unconscious: The History and Evolution of Dynamic Psychiatry.* New York: Basic Books, 1970.

Estes, W. K "Reinforcement in Human Behavior," *American Scientist,* 60 (Nov.-Dec., 1972), 723-729.

Estes, W. K "Is Human Memory Obsolete?" *American Scientist,* 68 (Jan.-Feb., 1980), 62-69.

French, John R. P., Jr., "A Formal Theory of Social Power," *Psychological Review,* 63 (1956), 181-194.

Gurin, G., Veroff, J., and Feld, Sheila. *Americans View Their Mental Health.* New York: Basic Books, 1960.

Hilgard, Ernest R. "Consciousness in Contemporary Psychology," *Annual Review of Psychology.* Palo Alto, CA: Annual Reviews Inc., 31 (1980), 1-26.

Horney, Karen. *Neurosis and Human Growth.* New York: Norton: 1950.

Humphreys, Christmas. *Concentration and Meditation: A Manual of Mind Development.* Baltimore, MD: Penguin Books, 1968.

Irwin, F. W. *Intentional Behavior and Motivation: A Cognitive Theory.* New York: Lippincott, 1971.

Jacobson, E. *You Must Relax.* New York: McGraw-Hill, 1957.

Janis, Irving, and Mann, Leon. *Decision Making: A Psychological Analysis of Conflict, Choice and Commitment.* New York: The Free Press, 1977.

Johnson, Donald K. *A Systematic Introduction to the Psychology of Thinking.* New York: Harper and Row, 1972.

Keller, Helen. *The Story of My Life.* New York: Doubleday, 1954.

Kimble (Ed.). *The Anatomy of Memory.* New York: Science & Behavior Books, 1965.

Koch, Sigmund (Ed.). *Psychology: A Study of a Science.* New York: McGraw-Hill, 1963, Vol. 5.

Lachman, Sheldon J. *Psychosomatic Disorders: A Behavioristic Interpretation.* New York: Wiley, 1972.

Lazarus, R. S. "Emotions and Adaptation: Conceptual and Empirical Relations," in D. Levin (Ed.), *Nebraska Symposium on Motivation.* Lincoln, NE: U. of Nebraska Press, 1968.

Mahoney, J. J., and Thoresen, C. E. (Eds.). *Self-Control: Power to the Person.* Monterey, CA: Brooks/Cole, 1974.

Mahoney, Michael J. "Reflections on the Cognitive-Learning Trend in Psychotherapy," *American Psychologist,* 32 (1977), 5-13.

Maltzman, Irving. "Motivation and the Direction of Thinking," *Psychological Bulletin,* 59 (1962), 457-467.

Mandler, G. *Mind and Emotion.* New York: Wiley, 1975.

McClelland, David C. "How Motives, Skills, and Values Determine What People Do," *American Psychologist,* 40 (1985), 812-825.

Meichenbaum, Donald, and Cameron, Roy. "The Clinical Potential of Modifying What Clients Say to Themselves," in Mahoney, M. J., and Thoresen, C. E. (Eds.), *Self-Control: Power to the Person.* Monterey, CA: Brooks/Cole, 1974.

Miller, G. A., Galanter, E., and Pribram, K. H. *Plans and the Structure of Behavior.* New York: Holt, Rinehart & Winston, 1970.

Mischel, Walter. "Toward A Cognitive Social Learning Reconceptualization of Personality," *Psychological Review,* 80 (1973), 252-283.

Mower, O. H. *Learning Theory and Behavior.* New York: Wiley, 1960.

Neisser, Ulric. *Cognitive Psychology.* New York: Appleton-Century-Crofts, 1967.

Neisser, Ulric. *Cognition and Reality: Principles and Implications of Cognitive Psychology.* San Francisco: W. H. Freeman, 1976.

Nezu, Arthur M., Nezu, Christine M. and Perri, Michael, G. *Problem-Solving Therapy for Depression.* New York: Wiley, 1989.

Norman, D. A. *Memory and Attention.* New York: Wiley, 1969.

Novaco, Raymond W. *Anger Control.* Lexington, MA: Lexington Books, 1975.

Parloff, Morris B. "Shopping for the Right Therapy," *Saturday Review,* (Feb. 21, 1976), 14-20.

Rolanyi, Michael. *Personal Knowledge.* Chicago: U. of Chicago Press, 1958.

Razran, J. *Mind and Evolution: An East-West Synthesis of Learned Behavior and Cognition.* Boston: Houghton-Mifflin, 1971.

Reitman, W. R. *Cognition and Thought.* New York: Wiley, 1965.

Salzman, Leon. *The Obsessive Personality: Origins, Dynamics and Therapy.* New York: Science House, 1968.

Schacter, Stanley. *Emotion, Obesity and Crime.* New York: Academic Press, 1971.

Schacter, S., and Singer, J. E. "Cognitive, Social and Physiological Determinants of Emotional States," *Psychological Review,* 69 (1962), 379-399.

Schneider, W., and Shiffrin, R. M. "Controlled and Automatic Human Information Processing: I. Detection, Search, and Attention," *Psychological Review,* 84 (1977), 1-66.

Simon, H. A. "Motivational and Emotional Controls of Cognition," *Psychological Review,* 74 (1967), 29-39.

Smith, Adam. *Powers of Mind.* New York: Random House, 1975.

Snaith, R. A. "A Clinical Investigation of Phobias," *British Journal of Psychiatry,* 114 (1968), 673-697.

Solzhenitsyn, A. *One Day in the Life of Ivan Denisovich.* New York: Dutton, 1963.

Spielberger, C. D., and DeNike, L. D. "Descriptive Behaviorism Versus Cognitive Theory in Verbal Operant Conditioning," *Psychological Review,* 73 (1966), 306-326.

Szasz, T. *The Myth of Mental Illness.* New York: Harpers, 1961.

Tinbergen, N. *Animal Behavior.* New York: Life Nature Library, 1965.

Valins, S. "The Perception and Labeling of Bodily Changes as Determinants of Emotional Behavior," in Black, P. (ED.), *Physiological Correlates of Emotion.* New York: Academic Press, 1970.

Walker, Stephen. *Animal Thought.* London: Routledge and Kegan Paul, 1983.

White, Robert W. "Motivation Reconsidered: The Concept of Competence," *Psychological Review,* 66 (1959), 297-333.

Wolfe, Joseph. *Psychotherapy by Reciprocal Inhibition.* Stanford, CA: Stanford University Press, 1958.

Wood, C. G., and Hokanson, J. E. "Effects of Induced Muscular Tension on Performance and the Inverted U Function," *Journal of Personality and Social Psychology,* 1 (1965), 506-510.

Yates, F. A. *The Art of Memory.* Chicago: U. of Chicago Press, 1966.

Young, P. T. "Hedonic Organization and Regulation of Behavior," *Psychological Review,* 73 (1966), 59-86.